THIS
COMMON
GROUND

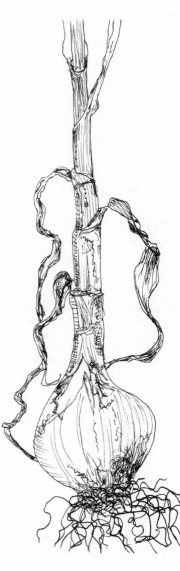

THIS
COMMON
GROUND

Seasons

on an

Organic Farm

SCOTT CHASKEY

VIKING

VIKING
Published by the Penguin Group
Penguin Group (USA) Inc., 375 Hudson Street, New York, New York 10014, U.S.A.
Penguin Group (Canada), 10 Alcorn Avenue, Toronto, Ontario, Canada, M4V 3B2
(a division of Pearson Penguin Canada Inc.)
Penguin Books Ltd, 80 Strand, London WC2R 0RL, England
Penguin Ireland, 25 St. Stephen's Green, Dublin 2, Ireland (a division of Penguin Books Ltd)
Penguin Books Australia Ltd, 250 Camberwell Road, Camberwell, Victoria 3124, Australia
(a division of Pearson Australia Group Pty Ltd)
Penguin Books India Pvt Ltd, 11 Community Centre, Panchsheel Park, New Delhi–110 017,
India
Penguin Group (NZ), Cnr Airborne and Rosedale Roads, Albany, Auckland 1310, New Zealand
(a division of Pearson New Zealand Ltd)
Penguin Books (South Africa) (Pty) Ltd, 24 Sturdee Avenue, Rosebank, Johannesburg 2196,
South Africa

Penguin Books Ltd, Registered Offices: 80 Strand, London WC2R 0RL, England

First published in 2005 by Viking Penguin, a member of Penguin Group (USA) Inc.

10   9   8   7   6   5   4   3   2   1

Copyright © Scott Chaskey, 2005
All rights reserved

In different form, "Serpent Garlic," "Smile, for Your Lover Comes," and "The Wolf's Peach"
first appeared in the *East Hampton Star*, East Hampton, New York.

Line drawings by Jessica Reynolds

Page 211 constitutes an extension of this copyright page.

LIBRARY OF CONGRESS CATALOGING-IN-PUBLICATION DATA
Chaskey, Scott.
        This common ground : seasons on an organic farm / Scott Chaskey.
        p.   cm.
        ISBN 0-670-03429-0
        1. Organic farming—New York (State)—Amagansett. 2. Chaskey, Scott. I. Title.
    S605.5.C456 2005
    630.5'84'0974725—dc22   2004061246

This book is printed on acid-free paper. ∞

Printed in the United States of America

for my mother, Mary

for Megan
and for our children,
Levin, Rowenna, Liam

𝄞 And when the fields are fresh and gree-een . . .

CONTENTS

THIS
COMMON
GROUND

. . . this sentient Earth

—*after* JOHN HAY

Well #1

#2

#3

#4

#5

#6

#7

#8

COMFREY

WETLAND

#9

#10

#11

#12

Oak Tree PLAQUE TO HONOR DEBORAH ANN LIGHT

HERB HERB

#13

#14 - #20

#21 - #29

Well Head

↓ 400 FT ↓

DEEP LANE

HARVESTSTAND

#34 #33 #32 #31 #30

YOUNG PLUM ORCHARD

BEE LOUD GLADE

HONEY BEE HIVE

YOUNG PEACH ORCHARD

APPLE ORCHARD

PRIVATE PROPERTY

TRACTORS

> THE VALLEY <

RASPBERRIES AND BLACKBERRIES #35

RHUBARB #36

#37

#38

#39

#40

— TRACTOR PATH —

COMPOST WINDROWS

NEWEST GREENHOUSE

LOWER GREENHOUSE

COLD FRAME

WIRE PEN

CHICKEN COOP

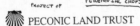

QUAIL HILL FARM MAP
BY SARAH

CAUTION: NOT DRAWN TO SCALE

PERENNIAL CROPS ARE LABELED

PROJECT OF

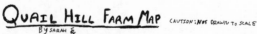

PECONIC LAND TRUST

SLEDDING HILL

TO FARM WORKSHOP

INTRODUCTION

In a peninsular place the clarity of light is partly what lures the lover of land and water. I have gardened and farmed on the Land's End peninsula of Cornwall and on the South Fork of Long Island, where the light, especially in spring and autumn, transforms the landscape. Soil, stem, branch, leaf, and fruit reflect the sea, and the farmer or gardener contemplates beauty and utility in one thought. I have learned to cultivate crops and poetic meter, and I admire the exercise of art, but wild nature is parent to each. Despite consistent schedules and plantings and cultivations, the fields I labor in continually yearn to return to a kind of natural chaos. I am fascinated to watch the order of succession in a field "let go." Once cultivated, the fields of Amagansett will sprout with an abundance of amaranth and lamb's quarters, followed by wild mustard, then miniature cedars and locusts, accompanied by a variety of grasses. In the fields we select to grow annual crops, by late spring as the soil warms I am literally surrounded by seeds, both indigenous and introduced, seeds breaking open, searching for light and nutrients. I am often overwhelmed, not uncommon for a gardener, by the force of April, or May, or June—but year after year I turn to observe and to admire the visitations of wind and water, the maturation of plants, the rebirth of seeds.

It was while living in Ireland and England, in the late seventies and the decade of the eighties, that I was captured by wood nymphs, piskies, the Queen under the Hill, the Green Man, and other ancient mythologies that flow from the soil. I lived for a time in and around Oxford, on the edge of the Cotswolds, where I learned how to handle a spade while digging vegetable gardens on Boar's Hill. I bedded down each evening in a "caravan" within a walled garden, and I assisted one Mrs. Darby with apple pruning, fencing, and repairs to the stone walls. Land was passed on within a carefully confined, if familial, set of rules, and opportunities to change the pattern of privilege were rare. I was initiated into gardening not by journeymen, but by craftsmen, and I learned—while pruning roses and double digging—the meaning of the word "character."

I remember an encounter on a narrow lane in Oxfordshire with an eighty-year-old Englishman who lectured me concerning the country life and the only two books worth reading—the Bible and Shakespeare. Quoting the Bard, useful advice for an apprentice gardener, he intoned, "Sweet are the uses of adversity, which like the toad, ugly and venomous, wears yet a precious jewel in his head . . ." (from *As You Like It*). And then he cocked his head and, for emphasis, stamped the turf and said, "Imagine the man thinking of a toad at that moment!"

The language of the garden and the language of poetry, for me, are inseparable. Emily Dickinson listened for the tune in the cricket's song, Gerard Manley Hopkins saw it in the hurl and glide of a kestrel, W. B. Yeats heard the bell beat of wings of "nine-and-fifty swans." While farming on the South Fork I have listened for the trill of the returning blackbirds in spring, I have seen the hedgerow ablaze in a late autumn light, a summer crop of buckwheat host a myriad of monarchs, a red-tailed hawk descend to a field to face a young red fox, a meadow of oats, millet, and peas rise to silver and green after a fresh rain. I am fortunate to carry with me to these fields some meadow knowledge, learned on the Penwith peninsula, mostly from one Cornishman who scampered about on stone pathways from garden to field to cottage throughout a long lifetime. I know now that it is helpful for a farmer to foster a character open—

in the words of the Wisconsin poet Lorine Niedecker—to both "tenderness and gristle."

My wife, Megan, and I lived for ten years in England, on a hillside above the tiny Cornish fishing village of Mousehole, in a collection of eccentric buildings, Love Lane Cottage, Love Lane Studio, and Green Hedges, once owned by the "bird ladies," Pog and Dorothy Yglesias, who maintained a correspondence with Megan for many years. The Yglesias sisters created a sanctuary—after villagers repeatedly brought them jackdaws and gulls—to heal and release injured birds. Megan, at age twelve, while living outside of Pittsburgh, Pennsylvania, was moved to respond to Dorothy's book, *The Cry of a Bird*, with a poem. The poem, hand-lettered by Megan, was there in Dorothy's dresser when we entered the cottage as caretakers fifteen years later.

We learned to shelter from the winds, to hide under a canopy of a Cornish hedgerow when the next shower arrived—usually at intervals of about fifteen minutes—and to recognize wild garlic, nettle, and narcissi pushing up out of dark soil and granite rock by the thousands and covering the unused cliff meadows with white sails. We also learned when to anticipate and to witness the sea of bluebells, brilliant and ethereal in the magical wood at St. Loy.

In 1989, while we were on an extended visit to the United States from England, my father-in-law, part of the original core of families uniting to form a fledgling community farm, asked me to come along to a Saturday meeting in the hamlet of Amagansett, New York. I was not preparing to leap from the steep cliff meadows of Mousehole to the flat fields of the South Fork, but I was welcomed back to the New World by the very strong sense of community in formation at that winter meeting. Perhaps it was natural—unscramble Scott Allan Chaskey, SAC, and there you have it, Community Supported Agriculture, CSA. The mantra reads: the community agrees to share the risks with the farmer. And underneath, and hidden, is the resurgence of a much broader community, one that includes the wind from the ocean, the woodland ferns, the return of the red fox, the fish hawk tilting above in the April air.

That same year Deborah Light, an Amagansett landowner and a lover of land, donated twenty acres of field and woodland to the Peconic Land Trust, which was founded in 1983. (She later gifted an additional 192 acres to the PLT.) John Halsey—whose ancestor made his home near the tip of the island in 1640—when presented with the concept, was very receptive to the introduction of a CSA farm on preserved land, land that consists of prime agricultural soils. The land trust had inherited land, and responsibility, so that a stewardship presence and plan were imperative. The CSA, formed two years earlier by the group of ten families, was actively searching for a secure land base.

While the stated mission of the PLT is to protect farmland and open space, the daily purpose of a community farm is to produce food, and to involve as many people as possible in that production and distribution. Since the land trust is a not-for-profit organization, part of its mission is to educate. Our farm is one of the original CSAs in the country, now part of a "movement" of perhaps 1,500 community farms scattered throughout the country. When I signed on as farmer I was one of four land trust employees; since that time the Peconic Land Trust has protected over eight thousand acres of land, and now employs twenty-five people. At Quail Hill Farm we now grow food for over two hundred families, and we supply food to restaurants, to a local school, and to food pantries. We maintain gardens for two local restaurants, and we mow surrounding fields or seed cover crops for various landowners and for other conservation organizations. Farm members visit the farm twice weekly from June through October to harvest food—they dig their own potatoes, fork their own carrots, pinch their own herbs, and cut their own sweet basil, rainbow chard, and tatsoi. Conservation and the practice of stewardship derive from our feeling for the land. As members of the farm walk and harvest in the fields they begin to recognize land as a community to which they belong.

As the farm has grown I have involved our community in social issues associated with agriculture and care of the land. For many years, as a certified organic farm, we have been part of the debate that culminated in the first national organic standards, recently implemented (the debate is far from over). Through meetings, letters, e-mails, and contact with other farmers, activists, and educators, we are involved in conversations that address our seed supply, food safety, distribution equity, and the spread of GMOs. Each of these issues demands serious and sustained attention; each begins with our focus on the health of the soil. For the farmer aware of ethical choice and ecological necessity, each flick of the hoe, each pass with the disc harrow, each disturbance of wild nature can also be an act that supports the integrity and beauty of the land.

Ultimately the glaciers, advancing and retreating on this land 20,000 to 60,000 years ago, inspired this book, as they also created the fine silt loam soil of Amagansett. This is a soil rich in minerals, and it contains, near the edge of the sea, the right ratio of sand and clay both to hold water and to let it pass through. Our fields rarely show even a pebble, a singular gift from glacier to farmer. Those who purchase a share in a community supported agriculture farm by definition share in the stewardship of that soil. Quail Hill Farm is in the best sense a communal response to the preservation needs of a seaside place, an attempt to create and conserve what Aldo Leopold, the author of *A Sand County Almanac*, calls "a state of harmony between men and land."

It is part of a poet's job to enchant, and to take upon himself the mystery of things, even if on occasion the object of inspiration comes in the shape of a hefty sack of compost. Above the cliffs of Mount's Bay, Edgar Wallis, who "tealed" the Cornish soil for over seventy years, taught me, above all, to sense in the natural music of a meadow what a seed or plant senses, to feel the interdependence of south wind, granite rock, mist, and a robin's chatter. One learns the trick of understanding the contract between land, sea, and inhabitant, as my teacher the Northumbrian poet Basil Bunting explained, by reading the wind, wave, and soil simultaneously with Yeats, Hopkins, Emily Dickinson, Bashō. My university mentor, Milton Kessler, spoke of the need for a writer to develop a believable speaking voice. What that was I did not know; but now, after years of study in the field, and as a member of a farming community, I have some idea of what he meant. It is one thing to recognize the power inherent in nature and in words, it is quite another thing to communicate it. In my daily work I encounter the essential beauty in a wet field of buckwheat, bellbeans, and clover, a flock of crows descending once again to devour the tomatoes, the voice of a small wren nesting in the lemon balm. Because my field of observation is also home to a community farm, the whole experience is open to others.

At the heart of every garden is the perennial cycle that I hesitate to name, "it is so near to the heart," of death and rebirth. Mythologies and cottage wisdom have always linked the span of a human life, or incarnation, with the mysteries of seasons and the soil. Lugging a Cornish cliff shovel down steep stone paths to the lower meadows, pacing the long rows of lettuce and root crops with a wheel hoe, heaving rye straw unto newly planted garlic cloves, I have seldom paused to consider the obvious metaphor. Rather, my account of life lived on a particular farm is a response to the gesture of a sea breeze or the slap of a rough wind, a language more clearly voiced by catbird or redwing in the cedars, or by the miniature English robin, territorial and eloquent, who would settle on the hilt of my cliff shovel, tiny talons to steel. In that instant, a word appears, as natural as butterfly weed or nettle. And I hear the Atlantic strike sand particle and rock, part of the ground we share, eventual soil.

PROLOGUE:
A WIND FROM THE SEA

In October of 1981, just after Megan and I settled in Cornwall, England, I happened to be puttering around in our hillside garden when I noticed that I was being watched, from above. I was diggging in the kitchen garden, which ran between the cottage and the studio, on a slope so steep that it was in fact difficult to stand. Love Lane, a narrow dead-end dirt track that gives access to the few cottages nestled into the granite hillside above the village of Mousehole, serves as a kind of observation post for visitors and for villagers out for a walk. One can survey the semicircle of stone cottages that rings the harbor and the thick harbor wall built in 1392, curved precisely to defend against southwesterly gales, or gaze twenty miles out toward the English Channel and the most southerly point of England, the Lizard Point. But Edgar Wallis was more interested in me, at work in the garden. He was peering through the hedgerow with an animal-like curiosity, rough hands parting the ornamental hedge of privet and fuchsia, a pair of eyes twinkling through the tangled branches. He wore a traditional cap that had seen some service and an old slicker draped over one shoulder, and he carried a basket filled with greenery.

"If you don't carry the soil up from the bottom and put 'im up top, she'll be mighty thin!" he called down. He was quick to read my puzzlement, so he soon continued his discourse, framed by fuchsia branches: "The meadow settles to the bottom . . . to do a proper job you must carry 'im up! 'Ere, I'll come down and show you. . . ."

This was the first of what would stretch into eight years of often daily conversations, as Edgar, returning from his meadows, would thrust himself into the hedge above the Love Lane Cottage garden, as the light was dying, and shout, "Scott! Where to?" I would always answer, whether I was down in the garden below Green Hedges, or tearing down or rebuilding one of the cottages, or attempting some poetry at my desk in the Studio. The day was not complete without Edgar's weather report, his advice concerning our crop of new potatoes, or a bit of song. He lived in the heart of the village, in the cottage in which his wife, Dora, was born. Each day he walked through the village alleyways, up the long streamside steps made of massive granite blocks, to "the mountains," and then along Love Lane to Raginnis, where the coast path continued toward Land's End and he descended to the cliff meadows to cultivate violets. He was nearing eighty when we first met, although he was careful to add a year or two whenever discussing his age. He was still as nimble as a fox when he climbed over the stiles that served like gates between fields, or when he scrambled down the stone steps built into the granite retaining walls surrounding each meadow.

Later, if we would chance to meet a group of visitors (from "up-

country" or the Continent, on holiday in the "Cornish Riviera"), on our way to and from the meadows, Edgar would happily pronounce, "From when I first met 'im, Scott and me fell in together!" In a landscape defined by tall granite walls everywhere, overarching hedges and branches, and narrow lanes best described as "roofless tunnels," I still marvel at the accuracy of his speech.

Through Megan's longtime correspondence and friendship with the two bird ladies of Mousehole, and through a fairy-tale twist of fate, we found ourselves the owners of an enchanted garden overlooking the historic fishing village, Mount's Bay, and a stretch of undulating coast known as "the earliest ground in Britain." Edgar was delighted to instruct me in the arcane arts of cliff gardening, as he was delighted to receive the benefits of an additional laborer. I soon learned of our good fortune to inherit a stand of pittosporum, planted by the bird ladies, and used as backing for flowers. My charming mentor taught me how to properly prune this ornamental tree, how to bunch and band together eight to ten stems, and to reject any leaves blackened by the east wind. Edgar and Dora's violets, packed in a shoe box, and my bunches of pittosporum, were transported weekly to Covent Garden, London, and we gardeners counted our pennies.

Edgar taught me the routes taken by fox and badger and rabbit, how to recognize the most fertile meadow soil, when to enter a meadow and when to "leave it be," how to select potato seed and when to sprout it, how to collect the shiniest ivy leaves for bunching. I knelt on the cliffs of the ancient duchy to receive, in lieu of a mantle or laurel crown, the tools of the trade: a sharp sickle, the long-handled shovel, and the curved chipper.

What I did not learn in Cornwall, where the mean temperature in winter is 48 degrees and the mean temperature in summer is 58 degrees, was a deeper knowledge of the seasons. In a moment of exasperated inspiration, after the "blackeaster" had assaulted us for almost two weeks, my wife renamed the seasons of western Cornwall: pre-rip, rip, and post-rip. The presence of palm trees and various subtropical plants in a climate influenced by the Gulf Stream is deceptive. Though the temperature is mild, the rains can be continual, and the winds, ferocious.

In 1989, when we relocated to the tip of another peninsula, the South Fork of Long Island, I was delighted to encounter a climate defined by a progression of four seasons, one where the sun is much more than an occasional guest. And it was soon imperative that I must gain more insight into that fickle and unpredictable variable, the weather.

Although new to the area, I quickly became involved with a group of people working to establish a community farm. The inspiration was a collective desire to create a reliable, local source for fresh organic food, and to encourage the practice of sound stewardship. At some point in the process, because of my horticultural experience, I was asked if I would be willing to be the head farmer. My reply: "But I know little about the local soil, the water cycles, and nothing about the seasons on the East End."

What you will read in this book is the education of a gardener become farmer, representing a committed community; the story unfolds within the broader context of a historic farming region. For one who works with the soil, all seasons eventually intertwine. But what follows is the record of a little more than a year on an organic farm, laced with the challenges faced by all small farms, enlivened by a wind from the sea.

When I first looked up into the Love Lane hedge to encounter the curious gaze of one vital Cornishman, I witnessed a man who spoke of plants as part of our family, who handled them with authority and tenderness, who knew the moods and feelings of plants as shown in leaves and roots. Years later, kneeling in another field to test some soil, I compare color, texture, and consistency with the soils of Mousehole's hillside meadows. With care, I carry a fistful of loam to the top of the field, where the tractor has left the soil a bit thin, and begin again.

SPRING

. . . In the first days of spring
when the untrammelled, all-renewing southwind blows
the birds exult in you and herald your coming.

—BASIL BUNTING,
"INVOCATION TO VENUS," 1927
(*translated from* LUCRETIUS)

SERPENT GARLIC

It is early in March. High up in an apple tree, as I am pruning within the canopy, my thoughts turn to the garlic cloves that have been bedded down for winter in an adjacent field. While I am in a rather precarious position, leaning on apple limbs, the garlic cloves, I know, are secure in that cold silt loam. Over the course of the winter the green shoots have stood like sails above a thick layer of straw mulch, waiting. Now as the days lengthen and the gardener thinks of seeds and seeding, the cloves of garlic, too, respond to increased light.

The reader may wonder—why does he begin with garlic? I have two responses—one quite practical and one most assuredly subjective. First, toward the end of winter when nearly all plant life prefers to remain dormant, there they are in the field—emerging from the cold soil, proclaiming "Primavera!"—the first sign of the color of spring, the self-confident shoots of the most potent of alliums. Second, I am in love with a plant that yearns for a friendship with each gardener through a succession of three seasons in the field, a plant shaped by personality and flavor.

Back at the farm shop our shelves are filled with bags and packets of other seeds, hundreds of varieties of vegetables and flowers to be, some already seeded in trays, warm and watered daily in the heated greenhouses. We are a cooperative farm—by name and by choice the farmers like to listen to members' desires. I began one farm letter to members with this: "We know that you are allium lovers. . . ." So each year we seed and seed again scallions and leeks, we plant over twenty-five thousand onion seeds, and in the autumn we place by hand twenty thousand garlic cloves in our best-tended soil. Each winter we devise new methods that will hopefully persuade members to postpone their harvest until these bulbs have matured. Even our most loyal members will forget principle and duck under the ropes to get to the alliums.

So let's talk about our favorite—*Allium sativum ophioscorodon,* known as hardneck or top-set garlic. This subspecies is easily distinguished from *sativum sativum,* or softneck, perhaps the more commonly known, by the spectacular twirling flower stalk that eventually sports a mysterious bulbil at stalk's end, somewhere in the air. Softneck garlic, on the other hand, is nonbolting; it will not produce a flower stalk. The bulbil, which is a kind of copy of the bulb maturing in the soil, will appear in early summer. Examine it and you enter into the mystery of this ancient plant. Garlic is asexual; it reproduces vegetatively through either cloves or the bulbils (top-set type). When we plant we place one clove in the soil, which will eventually produce a bulb. But a clove is actually a swollen leaf sheath formed to protect and nourish a bud. A clove is really a bulb within a bulb. And a bulb is not in the true sense a seed, it is a living plant. A bulb or a number of cloves sitting on your counter, or hanging in a braid, is waiting; botanists refer to this state as a period of rest.

Garlic probably originated in south-central Asia (the garlic crescent), and it has been cultivated for about five thousand years. Over the centuries it has been thought of as a source of physical strength, a cure for tuberculosis, arthritis, colds, and colitis. It possesses chemical properties that are antibacterial, antifungal, and antithrombotic. Allicin, a sulfur compound, is responsible for both aroma and medicinal effects. In the ancient world garlic was a food staple, but by the Middle Ages it had lost favor due to its inherent aromatic power. Increasingly, *Allium sativum* seems to be gaining new and uplifted social standing, perhaps for its "versatile flavoring ability." The essence of garlic is a volatile oil, also found to be effective as an organic pesticide. The Garlic Seed Foundation, long a source for practical and arcane information about this allium, includes in their logo an essential descriptive phrase, part of the character of the plant—"Food as Medicine."

Sometime around October garlic cloves want to return to the soil. They will grow in almost any soil, almost anywhere on the earth, but they adore a sandy loam rich in organic matter where no allium has had home recently. Good drainage is important; yields will be reduced by compaction, and lack of oxygen can lead to disease. In wet locations raised beds should be used. Garlic likes a pH of 6.2–7.5, so on Long Island we must add lime, at least a season before planting. One good grower actually prepares his garlic beds two years in advance. He starts with a cover crop of rye and clover, turns this in, then repeats rye, then grows two crops of buckwheat, a sure way to increase the organic content of the soil, and to improve the tilth. Tilth, a word I like because it describes a beneficent action of time, can be defined as the presence of good crumb structure, which allows for ease of tillage.

At planting time you must carefully open the garlic bulb, in order to divide the cloves. Most research has shown a direct correlation between the size of the planted clove and the size of the harvested bulb. Quail Hill Farm experience concurs with the scientific evidence. Thus, it is essential to search for good planting material. California Early, the large white variety found in most supermarkets, does not adapt well to the climate of the Northeast. We are fond of the hardneck varieties because of their superior flavor. Softnecks are reputed to store longer, but we have kept German White hard-neck through the winter and even into May of the following year.

Years ago, I discovered a large handsome garlic bulb displayed in an allium basket at our local health food store, and, after tasting it, I researched the origin. Someone's sister had worked at one Rattle-snake Ranch, in eastern Washington, and this gourmet garlic was the ripe result of that transcontinental connection. I called Rattle-snake Ranch repeatedly, until we eventually created a friendship. Nine years later I still look forward to my yearly conversations with Steve, the garlic man, and I am willing to adapt to his cultural intui-tion. Carpathian, the variety I first fell in love with, has not per-formed well in recent years in eastern Washington. We now welcome, in October, Steve's choice of German Brown and Spanish Rioja, which we know will adapt to the quite different environment of an island in the Northeast. Lately, we have discovered a German White hardneck grown by Gary Skoog in upstate New York, which performs beautifully down here on the island. It is slightly hot, full of flavors; it stores well; and each bulb offers five to six large cloves, easier on the chef, instead of the standard ten to fifteen cloves.

As an experiment, to complete a planting area when we run short of seed, I take a quick trip to the local supermarket, to purchase, from the produce section, a number of your average softneck garlic bulbs. I plant these cloves alongside our preferred hardneck variety, and we nurture each with equal affection. The softneck, probably from the region surrounding Gilroy, California, "the garlic capital of the world," although nicely formed, usually lack flavor, and a cer-tain insistence, characteristic of superior garlic, that vitality is here, within this very bulb. I return my focus to the top-set varieties.

We plant in late October (six weeks before a tough frost), in well-prepared soil, four inches apart in rows spaced twelve inches apart, the top of the clove planted twice the depth of the clove height. Cover with six inches of straw mulch or, better yet, well-chopped leaves. Wait.

Patience is a virtue without which a gardener is instead a mechanic. To understand the details is also necessary, but to enter into the invisible heart space of living plants, patience is a prerequisite. Garlic will be in the ground for nine months, and during this time you will visit often. In warm winters the first shoot will break through the mulch layer in late autumn. In early spring, even in the cold soil, garlic will send up its leaves, looking for more light. You will need to feed it once or twice with a good organic fertilizer to supplement the nitrogen. Lately we have added gypsum, a calcium supplement that garlic responds well to. The soil was previously fed with a liberal dressing of compost, at planting time. Pull any weeds that make it through the mulch. If you grow top-set garlic, it is time for another decision—whether to cut the acrobatic stalk (scape), which will produce the bulbils, or not. The debate is heated; garlic lovers are fanatical. One of the most knowledgeable, down-on-the-organic-farm experts, David Stern, would be shocked to read that I offer the grower an option. He claims that to leave the scape intact is to sacrifice 33 percent of the potential bulb growth. In any case, if you cut the twirling scapes when they are tender, you will be rewarded by the strong, juicy delicacy of green garlic—similar but superior to young scallions.

Sometimes we choose to admire the acrobatic stalks until the end. The chef at Nick and Toni's—they are farm members—loves to cook the tiny cloves that make up the bulbil. In June, the clove you planted will clone itself to form a bulb. By July, the bulb below is almost ready. When the leaf tips turn yellow, before the neck gives and causes the leaves to fall over, it is time to pull the plants. Traditionally, when only five leaves remain, the garlic bulbs are mature. Cure in the garden if you live in a dry place, or hang the bulbs in a dry, well-ventilated area for a few weeks. In the humid Northeast we are forced to hang our garlic to dry in the greenhouses, covered with shade cloth, fans set at full throttle. The first two weeks of drying time are critical. Those introduced to the sweet, strong taste of fresh garlic are often pleasantly surprised, though it is safest for all involved to taste together.

The ancient Greeks held that lovers of garlic would not be permitted to enter the temples of Cybele. We tell our farm members that if they are worried to be so easily dismissed, then better not to enter our temple of serpent garlic. Those unafraid are greeted by a sea of moons in groups of ten suspended from the metal hoop frames in the greenhouses for drying. If you crouch down, you are the planet receiving the (sulfurous) light of thousands of revolving cloves. Because garlic is in the ground for nine months, the grower of garlic has increased chances to develop an intimacy and, therefore, a knowledge. Once you become a true garlic grower, it is difficult to turn back, and intimacy with others may be another story. Again, have patience; invite any doubters to witness the twirling stalks of *ophioscorodon* gracing your garden, or the garlic moons later hanging to dry. This ancient food exemplifies a cooperation with wind, water, sun, and soil, leaves, seasons. The sweet smell of fresh garlic—medicinal, restorative—will prevail as a secret shared among friends.

SHINING FURROWS

Each day as I would pass by, where it rested on a slight rise of ground in our valley, I would remind myself, "We should have that ready to go before the start of spring." The John Deere disc harrow, which we trucked here from Pennsylvania years ago, is, at present, gathering a little rust at the end of the winter. It rests where we dragged it to at the very end of autumn, after part of the frame gave way in the field. At moments such as this I call upon my neighbor, who is employed at a nearby farm as the master of all trades. Luckily, as I was bicycling years earlier in and around Oxford, England, with purpose, devoting my afternoons to reading and writing in the Bodleian Library, John was learning how machines are powered, and how to weld. Although I can adequately repair a torn fuel line, or remove and replace a burst hydraulic hose,

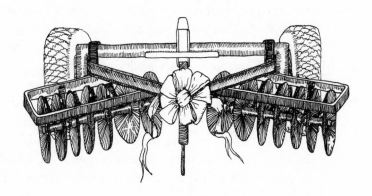

or mend a broken link in the chain that moves manure through the spreader, fusing metal to metal to make a joint is beyond me.

Recently, our son Liam, who had just been given his first lesson on the sewing machine by his mother, a superb seamstress, gently admonished me: "Dad, you should really learn how to sew!"

After thinking of my occupational history, both as professional and amateur, as a writer, housepainter, carpenter, book clerk, baker, cook, gardener, farmer, teacher, et cetera, I chose my words carefully, not to dampen my son's enthusiasm: "You know, Liam, there are certain tasks, at least in this lifetime, that I am happy to leave to others. It is a privilege to thank them for their expertise."

Welding is another of those tasks, though this does not diminish my pleasure in being witness to John's artistry. He arrived at precisely the right hour. A week previously, just as I was preparing to hitch up the chisel plow, which would be followed by the disc harrow, it rained, and continued for three days. Field work in the spring, especially involving the use of tractors, can be extremely tricky. The key—which I must relearn every April—is to watch for the window.

The window is here, and so is my neighbor, with the welding apparatus on the back of his pickup. He is patient, even with rough materials, the sign of a reliable artisan. We spend one half hour to find the correct alignment for the cast iron piece that carries the wheel. The workhorse harrow is made up of many discs (imagine metal dinner plates), four gangs mounted at opposing angles, to maximize the cutting power. The job of the disc harrow is to cut up the clods of earth, following the primary tillage, to prepare a seedbed. Hydraulics control the axle that holds the wheels; for traveling purposes, as the tires are lowered the discs rise, and in the field the action is reversed.

I hold the metal arm in place as John wields the rod of steel flux, and when he touches metal to metal, sparks fly. Fifteen seconds later, and after one bead of weld, we stand back. When the liquid steel cools down—from 1,200 degrees—John raps the axle and stands on the joint to test the first strength. The fusion of metal to metal, in the hands of a master welder, is remarkable. As the April sun and a strong wind from the ocean dry the soil, I stand back to watch the rest of the job. White light, a fluid heat, and sparks, like miniature shooting stars, brighten the cool air. We drop the hydraulic hoses from the Case tractor, approach the implement head on with the bucket loader, and ease the tongue of the disc up into a vertical position; now John can reach the underside of the joint. Within an hour the harrow is ready to go again; I hitch it up, and head for the soon-to-be pea patch.

Recently, in conversation with a local Episcopalian pastor, I learned for the first time of an old custom, one practiced, perhaps, by other farming cultures as well. Having been raised in a rural village in England, he revived the custom in his present parish in Bridgehampton, on the South Fork, to the surprise of a number of his parishioners. He pointed to an indented mark in the carpet on the altar, a mark where the plow had rested for a ritualistic "blessing of the plow." This was an annual ceremony in certain parts of England, done very early in the spring; the plow, after being blessed, was transported to the field wearing ribbons and garlands. And then the tool of steel was set to work, to break the earth.

There is a mystery at the root of this simple ceremony that I have no desire to uncover. But because I am still engaged as a plowman, I am intrigued by the details—the implements—of the story. I actually feel that the ritual enactment, on one hand a practical prayer for a good season, is also inspired by a cosmological reality— the planet Earth is born of stardust. The oldest elements we know, hydrogen and helium, were made inside stars—Earth was formed from these elements. The minerals that make up the matter that forms the frame and plowshares derive from the elements that left a parent star, somewhere in the cosmos, aeons ago. Ultimately, and more intimately than we would like to admit, we are connected even with the composite of steel that we employ to furrow the earth. I pursue this thought not to be frivolous, but as a means to understand what I feel when I stand back, after the first tillage, to examine the steel shanks of the plow. The surface rust, gathered over a winter under the trees, is worn away by the resistance of sand and clay after but a few passes, leaving a brilliant shining surface of steel designed to plow the earth.

I remember the promise of a Cornish cliff shovel, in exchange for hours of hard labor, a gift to be from Edgar Wallis, after a day of "turning ground." We climbed the old ship's ladder to his workshop; each day Edgar would prop these frail and faithful steps against a metal rod anchored in the stone of the barn, ten feet up, and then, at the end of the day, he would hide the evidence of entrance in a dark corner of the lower stall. The entrance door was on the second level of the old granite building, above the stone courtyard—so that without the ladder it appeared, oddly, as an entrance impossible to reach, leading nowhere. Edgar's storage room had the aroma of a badger's den—earthiness and human sweat combined with the damp that rises from granite. I looked to a few of the long-handled shovels leaning in the dark, each with a veneer of rust, and for a moment questioned my future. When Edgar grabbed one of the long handles and deftly spun the blade in and out of the invisible earth, describing, with Shakespearean grammar, the art of making a proper furrow, I believe I was hooked. The shovel and chipper that he used daily were wiped clean of soil, and oiled to prevent rust. The shine that I look for after the first pass with the chisel plow in spring, I first witnessed in the dark of a granite tool shed—a bit of light pierced through a hole in a tin roof, and glanced off the oiled steel share of the long-handled cliff shovel. Edgar flicked the blade, carving the imaginary furrow for the new potatoes, and chattered, " 'E'll last a lifetime, this steel blade . . . they don't make 'im like they once belonged to . . . and when 'e's worn we'll turn 'im over into a chipper!"

Carl O. Sauer, in his eloquent essay "The Agency of Man on the Earth," observes, "Wherever men live, they have operated to alter the aspect of the earth, both animate and inanimate, be it to their boon or bane." The English writer John Fowles comments, "All tools, from the simplest word to the most advanced space probe, are disturbers and rearrangers of primordial nature and reality—are, in the dictionary definition, 'mechanical implements for working upon something.' " Investigating the development of agriculture throughout the Western world, Sauer notes that " the oldest form of tillage is by digging." To till the earth is to alter it, whether digging by hand, with a stone, with a blade of steel fitted with a handle, or by pulling an implement through it, one fitted with a share, a moldboard, and colter, or several steel shanks fastened to an iron frame. According to the OED, to plow is "to obliterate by ploughing wrinkles." The plow itself is described as "an agricultural implement, used to prepare the soil for sowing or planting by cutting furrows in it, and turning it up, so as to expose a surface to the action of the air." The descriptive language implies respect, as should the practices of those who till. In the preliminary agricultural act— tillage, the one who tills or holds the spade, the plowman, must consider the future fertility of the field. Conventional practice has favored speed and increased horsepower. Sauer notes, "Spade and hoe and mixed plantings are an affront to our faith in progress. . . . Instead of going out to learn what (native) experiences and preferences are, we go forth to introduce our ways and consider backward what is not according to our pattern."

Two thousand five hundred years ago, in a chorus in *Antigone*, Sophocles paid homage to the plow. I still remember the elation I felt, reading this passage as a teenaged child of the suburbs, before having even lifted a spade full of soil; the connection I found through language was apparently tribal or ancestral.

The chorus sings,

The storm gray seas yield to his prows,
Earth, holy and inexhaustible, is graven with shining furrows
Where his plows have gone, year after year,
The timeless labor of stallions. . . .

It is not difficult to detect the hubris of the Western mind that wills "to have dominion over all the earth." But the poet chose his words with some thought, to celebrate the confluence of the elemental earth and us. Now we know that the earth is exhaustible, and the plow, capable of leaving furrows that catch the shine, is often an implement of obliteration.

Globally, we know of some soils that have been under continuous cultivation for over five thousand years (that's sustainability). In order to maintain those soils—and to restore others—I propose to alter the eloquent chorus imagined by Sophocles in a rugged land, long ago. The passage quoted above, deep in my memory, begins: "Numberless are the world's wonders / But none more wonderful than man." With my mind on the bright blade of the cliff shovel and the clean shank of the chisel, I suggest, "And one of the wonders is man." My thought is to include the elements that left faraway stars billions of years ago, and billions of unseen organisms within the furrow. In chorus with the sun, they create the shine.

"NOTHING IS SO BEAUTIFUL AS SPRING"

Elizabeth Bishop begins her book *A Cold Spring* with this: "A cold spring . . . / For two weeks or more the trees hesitated; / the little leaves waited, / carefully indicating their characteristics." I am reminded of her observation this April, as we all wait. But as the days grow longer and the soil warms, our farm begins to hum again. On the first day we were able to work the cold soil, myself and fellow farmer Tim L. found a handful of fertility left by our winter cover crop of oats and hairy vetch in the valley. The roots of the vetch, a legume, exposed by our chisel plow, were loaded with the nodules that supply future food for our plants. This was a classic example of a "green manure"; the pink liquid within the root nodule indicates that nitrogen has been organically fixed in the soil. We plowed in the oats and vetch, which held the soil through the winter, to add plant matter to the field.

It is our practice, when we sow the cover crops in autumn, to add some legume seed to the grain (generally oats or rye). This is a traditional method to ensure that a farmer continues to build and maintain a fertile growing soil. The alternative, because plants need nitrogen, is to purchase a fertilizer high in nitrogen, and the tendency is to use more and more of it. Conventional agriculture, or monocultural farming, which became the dominant methodology after World War II, is based upon the use of these soluble salt fertilizers. Initially, crop yields grew exponentially, and farmers were finally able to look forward to some predictable results. However, resorting to synthetic fertilizers, in order to supply three of the essential nutrients—nitrogen, phosphorus, and potassium (NPK)—eventually leads to an overall breakdown of soil structure. The use of nitrogenous fertilizers reduces organic matter in the soil, which diminishes the soil's ability to hold moisture and to retain nutrients for the benefit of plants. The soil can become, quite literally, lifeless. Yes, plants may continue to perform in such a growing medium, if fed with an increasing ration of these macronutrients. (The list of macronutrients, those used in greatest quantities by plants, also includes carbon, hydrogen, oxygen, calcium, and sulfur.) After a time the results of such a "fast feeding" method have proven to be disastrous. Soil without life, reduced to a powder, will be lost to erosion, by wind or water. Soil without structure is a dwelling without a foundation. And we want to encourage billions of microorganisms to dwell in our soils.

Nitrogen, one of the big three, constitutes about 78 percent of our atmosphere. However, atmospheric nitrogen (N_2) is not much use to plants, which can use only nitrogen that has been destabilized by bonding with oxygen or hydrogen. During World War I a German chemist, Fritz Haber, discovered a method that could produce a plant-usable nitrogen (NH_3). This chemical process requires great amounts of heat and pressure in order to alter the bond in atmospheric nitrogen. For instance, the energy from burning 2,200 pounds of coal will produce 5.5 pounds of usable nitrogen. So the production of synthetic fertilizers requires massive use of fossil fuels. In recent years crop yields—the standard figures used to support conventional farming methods—have continued to diminish. This is an unforeseen result of what was proudly labeled the "green revolution," a methodology that allowed fewer farmers to manage greater acreage, and to purchase fertility as a commodity. The biological reserves in our soils, which are the true measure of fertility, are now impoverished, after years of trusting chemical analysis rather than a reading of biological cycles.

True fertility in soil is the result of a dynamic, complex interaction among minerals, animals, fungi, microorganisms, and plants. There are apparently billions of live organisms in a cubic foot of healthy humus. I am in love with this undiscovered country, and I am strangely encouraged by the words of the naturalist John Hay: "And for all the information we try to gather, we are only surface dwellers looking in on an unfamiliar universe."

I prefer the holistic approach to farming, which has deeper roots in this century than you might guess, and much deeper roots, of course, if one considers the previous ten thousand years of agricultural history. Sustainable farming techniques have long included the use of leguminous plants—peas and beans—which capture nitrogen from the air, and make it available to other plants by a fixation process within the soil. Bacteria and other microbial life increase through symbiotic relationships, and soil health improves as nutrients are stored and released to the benefit of plant life.

I have seen evidence of soil exhaustion, close up. When we took over farming the field we call "hurricane hill," there was not a worm to be found in the full five acres. Though the result was not intended by the hardworking farmer who managed this field before us, the monocrop rotation of potatoes, corn, potatoes, corn, potatoes, et cetera, nourished by synthetic fertilizers, drained the life out of the soil. The only significant life turned up by our tiller was an alarming number of grubs, at home in the anaeobic soil conditions. Our first-year attempts at vegetable production had meager results. I distinctly remember a number of original farm members, perhaps encountering this Oriental staple for the first time, exclaiming, "Why do we have row after row of daikon radish? And what do we do with it?"

The truth is daikon worked in our diminished soil; many crops, including simple-to-grow greens, faded away into the saddened Amagansett loam after the seeds had sprouted.

This spring, fifteen years later, I am pleased to report that in the same field, in our improved soil, daikon is accompanied by Easter egg radish, arugula, ruby chard, broccoli rabe, mizuna, tatsoi, spinach, assorted lettuces, and hakurei turnips. Tender new kale and collard leaves sprout on the treelike stalks of last year's plantings, which have overwintered. Before the brassicas go to seed, as they will the following spring, we can taste the sweet leaves of these plants that love the cold. The valley is now beginning to resound with the returning birds. Turn at the end of a row of raspberry canes and you will witness a double purpose—the sparrows have found a new perch.

A late April rain falls on the oak and beech leaves, the bright red Lely weeder, and on the narcissi and double daffodils on the bank. Awakening life is revealed through the variety of colors—the iridescence of the bluebird, the emerald of moss on stone, the light brown buds on tendrils of beech, a red haze over the apple orchard. All of this is the signature of Ariel's season. We're planting seeds now, by the thousands, and we anticipate shoots and first leaves to unfurl from soil, to touch the air and take on color. I will close with the line by Gerard Manley Hopkins that begins Bishop's *A Cold Spring*. As I feel the bite of the wind from the Atlantic, I recognize that a poet's cadence is selected from syllables indigenous to a season. Hopkins wrote, "Nothing is so beautiful as spring."

NESTS EVERYWHERE

We find nests everywhere; placed neatly in the herb garden under the hyssop as it greens, tucked by a wren into the towel dispenser by the chicken coop, and in the obvious and appropriate setting, the crook of apple limbs. When I went to take down the bicycle left to hang for the winter from the tall shed roof, I couldn't—a sparrow had nested in the upside-down basket attached to the handlebars. We had to pause while mulching the rhubarb—one of the earliest crops to mature—because a wren had built her nest under a roof of massive rhubarb leaves. Joe G., a farm member, anticipating nests, placed two bluebird boxes in the wild area between apple orchard and farm field. The boxes, which are drilled with the exact entrance hole preferred by bluebirds, rest on top of a four-by-four that is armored with a metal raccoon guard. The hope is that a pair of tree swallows take up residence in one box, a pair of bluebirds in the other. Joe visits often; with a screwdriver he carefully opens a side panel of each box to check for progress. If sparrows have taken over—they tend to be aggressive—he per-suades them to leave. Bluebirds are in need of our assistance. I recall Joe's radiance on the day he dis-covered four eggs in bluebird box number two—he echoed the April song of the nesting birds.

The Reverend Bill Chase, no longer with us, was so sensitive to the birds of Quail Hill that he ordered two cedar feeding trays, which we mounted on hickory posts near the bluebird boxes. Bill would retrieve eggshells at Estia, a friendly local restaurant very supportive of the farm; then he would carefully crush the shells, and deposit them as an appetizer for our entire winged population. When he noted that birds were at first hesitant to dine, Bill encouraged myself and the Quail Hill workers to crouch in the underbrush and practice our trills and whistles. On good days these trays now attract assorted traffic, lured by shells and organic sirens.

The Reverend Chase was an original member of the CSA, and probably our senior member. I have a memory of his deliberate, slow descent toward the ground in search of the perfect green beans to harvest for supper. He spent his weekdays in Manhattan, still thinking of the farm in Amagansett. His were the last letters I received—often on a weekly basis—to be plunked out on a trusty portable typewriter. With the first epistle, I recognized the font and the characteristic variation in imprint; I'm sure Bill composed on the same model that I carried off to college and then to France and England—an Olivetti Lettera 22. I kept Bill's letters in a file labeled "Correspondence," until it filled to overflowing; I followed this with the only sleeve in the cabinet to bear an individual's name—"Bill Chase." He came to be known as the Quail Hill master of sprouts, because of his love for the tiny cabbages on a stalk. He was known to venture out into a January field just to recover a few sprouts coated with ice. Here is his commentary:

> I made it on New Year's Day, and with a sort of militant determination to "make up." Snow was five or six inches deep. Not a track in sight anywhere—save those of two parked vehicles. I headed straight for Brussels Sprouts area, and tried, mindful of your instructions long ago, to break off those small very frozen miniature cabbages. My fingers got VERY cold and my nose kept

running as I bent over, and since no one else was anywhere in sight, I remembered that oddly enough I happened to have my pruning saw with me. It worked very
easily—on four stalks. Many discarded leafs left there to
replenish etc. Bill

Brussels sprouts are set out as transplants in late July, so as to mature in very late autumn. In England, sprouts are timed to be ready
for Christmas dinner. Like collards, they need a few good frosts to
sweeten or, at the very least, some extended cold weather. So back-
track about five weeks, and the time to seed brussels sprouts in
trays, at least on the South Fork, is in mid-June. Now that is a very
busy time of year on a mixed vegetable farm. One year we forgot to
seed the sprouts. By the time I realized the oversight, it was too late.
We had a great debate concerning who would drop the news to the
Reverend Chase. In the end, we were all cowards.

When Bill finally approached me, he was only mildly concerned.
"I know you rotate all the crops, each year, but I can't seem to find
the sprouts. I just want to commune with the plants I adore, and offer my respect and support."

Backing away (there's always some other work to be done on a
farm), I muttered, "Uhh, Bill, we, uh, with the best intentions, you
know, and we do have a lot of crops to think about . . . well, we like
sprouts, too, but, well, we sort of forgot to plant the seeds this
year."

That was a singular mistake at Quail Hill Farm. I do recall another year, however, when, out on a tour of inspection, Bill learned
that the sprouts had been planted adjacent to the farm stand, the
place where all members pause before they begin to harvest. I received a note from the reverend: "I'm a little concerned about the
accessibility."

Bill could be very vocal, also, concerning the crops that he
viewed as useless—usurpers of space that could be better devoted
to brussels sprouts. His letters often contained a newspaper article

to flush out his intent. In the final paragraph of an article included in one such letter, entitled "A Fancy Food Store Now Stresses the Food over the Fancy," he had underlined "Escarole didn't sell at all, neither did collards. . . . The most spurned vegetable was rutabaga."

His Post-it, for emphasis, simply stated, "Scott: Please NOTE CAREFULLY underlined portion in clipping. Vox populi, vox Dei, sez I. Bill Chase."

The days are still cold, and the sky is often overcast, so spinach and peas and early greens are beginning to come on in the field, but slowly. At one time I would rush to plow the first ground, and hurry to get those first seeds in. At that time I was unfamiliar with the cold springs that characterize the tip of this island. Until the water warms, we are still wearing layers. Recently I reread a number of springtime letters that I had addressed to our farm members. In nearly every letter I had used a variation of this line: "Spring is later than usual this year, so we are two weeks behind in our first plantings. . . ." Now I ask, later than what, or when?

The choice of when to open up the ground is more of an instinct (a restless one) than a calculated decision. I find it difficult to articulate my reasoning to the apprentices; I simply know when it is time to hook up the chisel plow, and to create the first furrow. As I continue to farm I encounter the complexities involved in the interrelation of soil, water, wind, and light. The marriage of instinct and experience is difficult to communicate, but essential to master.

The earliest crops to be direct-seeded—spinach, peas, and fava beans—love to go into a cold soil. But if two weeks of wet weather and 30-degree nights follow the planting, the seeds will not open up. And a worse scenario is possible—they could fail in the ground, before germination. It is for this reason that I prefer to wait, at least until the soil temperature rises by a few degrees. On the other hand—and this is the story of farming—if these cold-tolerant crops are seeded too late, when the weather warms they will lose vigor all too quickly, and fade into the haze of warm afternoons.

Since winter turned to the late March days when the soil does begin to warm and light lingers, we have pruned, seeded trays for the greenhouse, turned some soil, added compost and mulch, knelt in the returning green. The tightly curled leaf and stalk of rhubarb, a perennial, continues to unfurl from what is left of last year's mulch. We are cutting the canes of the ever-bearing raspberries to the ground, and spreading straw to keep down any weed growth among the crowns and the new canes beginning to sprout.

When we planted the peas, we first made a furrow, and then sowed the peas in a wide band, to ensure multiple germination and an eventual thick hedge of pea vines, which now begin to reach up over the trellis. I cultivated, a few times, with the Case cultivating tractor, to clean the aisles, before we began the process of staking and trellising. After that, access by tractor is blocked, and the only traffic, we hope, is the human animal.

I'm grateful for the abundance of sugar snaps and Mammoth Melting snow peas, including a massive weight of vines—but how to prevent the vines from entwining into a mass of impenetrable greenery? Once one row has found the row opposite, originally planted at a distance of five feet, center to center, the gardener has lost. When the vines are mature, we've learned to visit the pea patch once a day and to draw the greenery back toward the trellis with lengths of sisal or hemp. The vines of Mammoth Melting will continue to ascend to seven feet or more, and will produce until the onset of real summer heat. Meanwhile, the more compact vines of shucking peas, which we let tumble in a row on the ground, will keep producing almost as long. When harvested young, the shucking pea Green Arrow is the sweetest we have found.

We've moved on to the second or third planting of greens, still in search of the delicate taste of spring. Flea beetles, minuscule and fast, love to dine on the brassicas and the young oriental greens, also

looking for the delicate taste of spring. We will till up the first plantings of mizuna, arugula, broccoli rabe, red mustard, cress, and clay-
tonia after the beetles have had their fill, probably to follow those
early plantings with a summer cover crop of buckwheat. The soil
will benefit from more matter, and the bees will be in ecstasy.

Passing the wild patch in the middle of our valley, where the
hives are kept, I see that the bees are busy at midday, flying up and
over the patch of early greens. When we exchange the greens for
buckwheat, we will shorten their flight; they will work that crop as
long as it flowers, and the shorter the flight, the greater the store of
honey they can create. On the edge of the wild patch, the Reverend
Chase's eggshell feeding stands stand empty. It's time to fill them, in
memory of Bill:

> Weekend weather provoked high energy level for
> me . . . and hours washing and pounding egg shells! Por-
> tions of the white left inside shells hardens into a film—
> to which egg fragments adhere even when pulverised. I
> discovered however that soaking as well as washing helps
> loosen fragments from film—and that if left untended
> for a while then stirred, the film pieces float to top—and
> can be discarded. I'll be very disappointed if we learn
> that birds like the film! Warm best wishes to you,
> Bill Chase

Before leaving for the day I stop at the robust rhubarb plants that
we transplanted to the valley two springs ago. I'm here to check on
the mother wren. Earlier, mulching the rhubarb with Karen G., as
we leaned into the canopy, she exclaimed, "Look—a nest!" There
they were—four tiny speckled eggs nestled among the rhubarb stalks
in what for a bird that size must have the appearance of a tropical
jungle. When the eggs hatch the young will look up to a dark canopy
of veined green broken only on occasion, when we harvest from the
forest. When we approach the center of the rhubarb row we will cut

with care until the wrens fledge, and the nest will then serve as a gift of mulch, left by another Quail Hill resident.

In the morning I will check for the progress of chicks in wrens' nest number two—the one suspended from the rafters in the metal basket attached to a Peugeot bicycle. Luckily, the nest was made directly above the parking place for our Case 265 tractor. The seat makes a perfect platform for the curious inspector. So write this into a farmer's job description: witness to nests. I am reminded of this line by George Oppen: "There are things we live among, and to see them is to know ourselves."

"TEELIN' TATIES"

At the start of spring I project my singing voice to the top of the cedars, where the red-winged blackbirds rest and trill, and I let loose, rising on the final word: "And when the fields are fresh and gree-een . . ." This is the melody I associate with Edgar Wallis, which he intoned in passing, on his way to or from "the mountains," to plant or cultivate or pick violets, the winter flower. I was often reminded that this traditional song was "'eard in London and on the BBC," performed by the Mousehole male choir, with Edgar in residence in the tenor section. Raised in a family of fishermen, in a council house set just above the granite shoreline, Edgar was proud to claim his independence: "I took to the land!"

For years Edgar labored in the meadows carved into the cliffside, and also in the upland fields, "teelin' taties." I was told that two men could move faster than a machine through the field, planting the premium crop of early spring, new potatoes. In England, and on the Continent, the first potatoes harvested are considered to be a delicacy. Because Cornwall is the sunniest spot in England (a relative term to be sure), and because the meadows just to the west of Mousehole face southward, the first potatoes from mainland Britain to appear in London each year are harvested from this headland, "the earliest ground in Britain." Once Edgar guessed that I fancied the whole escapade of cliff gardening, new potatoes became the prime topic of discussion from late summer, through autumn and the late winter planting, until harvest, the following spring.

"We 'ave to set 'em out early, before anyone 'as the idea, really, that's how it belongs to be done—set 'em out early in trays to sprout, and get 'em in the ground first thing, before the others."

Early meant sometime in November—potatoes purchased at Cornwall Farmers, and roughly yet lovingly placed, one by one, in wooden vegetable trays rescued from the greengrocers. The sprouting trays were left in a place safe from frost, out of direct light, in order to nurture stubby, strong sprouts from the tuber eyes, which would later break through spring ground and broaden into mature potato plants. The gardener kept his eye upon the seed until sometime into the new year, when the ground was ready to "teal over." It was common to break ground in January, and on occasion seed potatoes could be set out at the end of the month. Generally, planting took place in February, as the narcissi began to emerge and blossom in the wild along the pathways, and out of the granite walls. What a difference a warm ocean current can create. Although eight degrees north of New York City, the Penwith peninsula rarely feels a frost, and palm trees (distinctly Nordic in character) line the streets of Penzance.

The hedges that surround and protect the cliff meadows are filled with flowers. Most of these are the legacy of market gardeners who tended the meadows in a productive time, in the years leading up to World War II. A stunning selection of bulbs, rejected and chucked into the nearby hedge by flower growers, or over a stone fence, now provides cascades of color in the wild verges, often framed by massive granite blocks bleached gray and green and white. At the end of an afternoon of turning ground or planting, I would wade among bramble and fallen privet branches to cut the evening's bouquet. Our cottage was filled with the fragrant gift of some peak years of bulb production on the headlands of the Penwith peninsula.

We made a furrow with the traditional long-handled cliff shovel, moving up the steep slope, and laid the seed potatoes one foot apart within the trench. The soil removed to form the next furrow serves to cover the seed in the previous furrow, and so on, as the gardener plants from fuchsia hedge to stone wall, until the meadow is complete with seed, from stone hedge to stone hedge. Many gardeners and farmers conduct a lifelong pursuit for the formal perfection also named "beauty." Captivated by the euphoria of a favorable season, all gardeners would nod in recognition of John Keats's, "Beauty is truth, truth beauty . . ." Emily Dickinson, writing at the end of Keats's century, and in a more pragmatic (American) fashion, states, quite simply, "Beauty is Nature's fact." The brief fallow time that follows potato planting illustrates this concept. The freshly turned chocolate soil, fluffed up by the shovel, settles slowly, and a fine geometric pattern reveals itself—rounded ridges of soil cover the seed potatoes, without a blemish of a weed, from ornamental hedge to solid stone. The scene remains undisturbed, except for occasional paw prints, for a good two weeks, which is unusual in the game of growing things.

From seed piece to potato plant to mature tubers can be a twelve- to thirteen-week process, equal to one quarter of a year, or, in other words, a season. The potato plant that sprouts from the seed tuber grows at a rapid pace, produces flowers, then, as the energy is transferred and the new tubers form, the plant dies back, and is reduced to a sheet of compost on the surface of the soil. In Cornwall the very first potatoes were prized, and because they fetched a premium, we planned for an early harvest. In fact, Edgar would spy upon his nephew, a "boy" of sixty-five, in anticipation of the first harvest of spuds. Imagine the price per pound if we could dig a day or two before the boy!

At Quail Hill Farm we grow between fifteen and twenty varieties yearly, and we traditionally harvest the Red Golds within twelve to fourteen weeks. Following that, we harvest a succession of varieties—Yellow Finn, Russian Banana, Ozette, All Reds and All Blues, Bintje, Coastal Russet, Carola, and Kennebec, to name a few. We harvest from mid-July into November, a luxury that again is the result of warm ocean temperatures. The last spuds are harvested in the cold and transported immediately to our root cellar, where they will store until May. In Cornwall, in mild and wet conditions, tubers, if left in the ground, would begin to sprout again. At such a point potatoes usurp management of men, even though we plan for the reverse.

Potatoes were not always considered a respectable food for human consumption. First cultivated in the Andes of South America, where the International Potato Institute now stores genetic stock from thousands of varieties, the potato found its way to Spain in the early 1500s. Europeans in general were suspicious of this member of the nightshade family, and not until the tuber was embraced by the Irish, late in that same century, did the New World plant begin to take hold. Although grains were difficult to grow in the cool, wet climate of the Emerald Isle, the potato flourished. It took nearly another two hundred years for the "bread root" to find acceptance throughout Europe, and this was not without coercion. Frederick the Great of Prussia offered his people the choice of planting potatoes or having their ears cut off. In 1719 some Scotch-Irish immigrants brought the humble spud to the North American continent, to Derry, New Hampshire. Throughout its circuitous route of travel, a single feature of the tuber from the Andes, despite persistent suspicion, eventually won the day—the potato could produce more food energy per acre than wheat, rice, or corn. To complete the picture of global expansion, today Russia and China produce more potatoes than any other country in the world.

Stubbornly, we still plant spuds by hand at Quail Hill. The soil is prepared with tractors—the cover crop plowed in and disced, then a seed bed made smooth with a harrow followed by a spindle roller. Then a furrow is cut through the clean soil, and our homemade dibbler, which is quite neolithic in appearance, is rolled in the depth of the furrow to mark the sequence for seed potatoes, roughly twelve inches apart. Three thousand pounds of seed, which arrive in early April from Moose Tubers (a Maine cooperative, of course), have been sorted and cut and cured for several days or a week, awaiting the optimum spring conditions for planting. Our potato dibbler is the handiwork of Timothy Laird, a former star of the mound, whose spud-in-the-hand to dibble-in-the-furrow coordination remains unrivaled. Others have tried, but only sporadically can we, in one fluid motion, propel the seed potato from an upright, walking stance, so that each seed piece sticks in the furrow in proper order. I'm good at it, but my foot is there to correct an errant pitch. Tim is a master of this motion, performed with considerable humor and much more grace than a mechanical transplanter would have. His style improved after a term in Bolivia with the Peace Corps, where he discovered the custom of uttering one word, *Pachamama!,* as an earthy prayer to bless each seed piece planted. As a responsible supervisor I had to discourage Tim from completing the Bolivian custom. With each cry of *Pachamama!* the Andean potato planters would cleanse their palate with a shot of white lightning, perhaps fermented from a previous harvest.

The potatoes are covered, and progressively hilled—soil is tossed up from either side by rotating steel discs—with each cultivation, to protect the tubers that swell out of the root structure, and will attempt to break through the soil before truly mature. The actual potato plants, which rise from the eyes of the seed pieces, progress into a branching treelike structure, resplendent with flowers before dying back. In the interim the wise farmer must daily monitor his crop, especially to detect the first appearance of an ubiquitous pest, the Colorado potato beetle. When I tended the meadows in Cornwall I never gave a thought to *Leptinotarsa decemlineata,* except when I passed by the oversized posters prominently displayed at immigration, warning against the importation of this pesky beetle. On Long Island, where at one time over seventy thousand acres of potatoes were under cultivation, this insect with its ravenous hunger for the potato plant (and more so, for eggplant) is a visitor to every field, and winters well in each hedgerow that surrounds our farm. This slow-moving spotted beetle the size of a raisin raises great fear in those who grow spuds. One of the last remaining potato farmers on the South Fork decorates the doors of his farm truck with an over-sized Colorado potato beetle in a conquered position. It is remarkable that the chosen means of locomotion for this prolific, persistent insect is by her own six legs. She is not adept at staying airborne.

In the first years of the farm, when we planted but a couple hundredweight of seed potatoes, we attempted to control the CPB by hand-picking, dropping the scrambling beetles into yogurt containers. By the time we completed one row, the first plants were covered again with spotted insects, and those caught were piggybacking up, over, and out of the Stonyfield container. It is difficult to maintain a positive morale in a farm crew against such odds. We gave up, and accepted diminished yields. Left to forage and to reproduce, the CPB will completely strip a field of plants. The larvae, who are the actual ones who dine, devour the leaves that provide food for the spuds. Over the years, as we increased our plantings, we recycled the yogurt containers and purchased a sprayer. Although rotations and other preventative methods confuse most insects, in the potato country of Long Island, the CPB is a persistent reality. Under organic standards, prior to the National Organic Program ruling, it was allowable to spray BT, *Bacillus thuringiensis,* a soil-borne bacteria suspended in solution. BT immobilizes the stomach of the larvae, but itself breaks down immediately in the environment. Depending on the year, one to four applications of BT, which is not a broad-spectrum insecticide, is calculated to reduce the population to a manageable tribe, so that potato plants will flourish.

The beetle in such abundance is a potent sign that the natural balance of a bioregion is upset. Many years of potatoes, potatoes, and more potatoes (on Long Island, in Idaho, Maine, the Dakotas) are an invitation to the insect population searching for an abundant food source, or nourishment, just like us. I love potatoes and admire the layered history of a wild crop that satisfies human need, arising out of the difficult conditions of a South American mountain range. A farm member once asked, "Why is it that we always have such an

amazing and prolific supply of potatoes, in all shapes and colors?"
My answer: "My mother is Irish." But it is also a food crop that
raises a flag; and we should respond with respect, cultural restraint,
and moderation in our use of this plant.

The harvest season extends from late July into November. One
year, harvesting potatoes at Thanksgiving, our fingers breaking
away shards of ice, I watched a scurry of bluebirds, ten or more—
the only time I have seen such a display—pause in the field for their
final harvest before heading south. Our final harvest of the year was
saved from frost by a few inches of good silt loam.

For years I have taken pleasure in the production of potatoes,
second only to the pleasure of eating them. Yet, overproduction and
improper rotations continue to be harbingers of disaster, and such
practices are quite simply the result of man's hubris. My ancestors,
and yours, probably, suffered terribly due to a lack of foresight concerning one cultivar (and the landlords' lack of compassion). There
is an alternative. Visit Quail Hill and we will share the harvest with
you—of French Red Fingerlings—grown and tested in fields on a
few continents, raised with organic methods in a Long Island field at
one time overstuffed with potatoes. This same field is now prepared
with sufficient cover crops, compost, and crop rotations to create a
healthy meal of spuds, delicate and full of flavors supplied by the
soil of the Andean mountains, the plains of Burgundy, the tundra of
northern Maine, and the Atlantic shoreline of the South Fork.

THE INVISIBLE STRING

The fox den has been empty for several years now; should I simply drag the chisel plow over the abandoned hole and follow with a disc harrow, returning what was a home to a seedbed for row crops? This was my thought in April when I went out to plow our far field. We have shared a part of this field with a certain fox family on and off for about ten years. One spring, after opening up some new ground, I stood back to admire the freshly turned soil. What I came to recognize as the nose of a fox hesitantly emerged from the clods—or was it a pair of noses? And what were they doing digging from underground, here, just where this year's squash patch was to be planted? I had never given it a thought—is it possible to share an agronomic field with a fox?

I turned to other spring work, giving Madame Renard a chance to alter her plans. I was hopeful that on return I would find the burrow abandoned; surely the three hundred acres of woodland to the north was a wiser place to raise a family. Why would a self-respecting fox choose a site a mere fifty feet from a paved, well-traveled road, and in a field traversed by tractors, farm wagons, and workers? I found, instead, evidence of digging in—a mound of earth leading to the perfect circle of an entrance hole, and the delicate prints of padded feet. Gingerly, I leaned to inspect the entrance. Within, not far from the surface, I could see the shape of a very large water conduit pipe. She had chosen for her home a place adjacent to the drainage viaduct that snakes through this field, part of a county engineering project to improve water runoff. She must have found in displaced soil an ideal location for a den. But why so near to vehicular and human traffic? Was this a site chosen by foxes prior to human habitation? Whatever the reason, this South Fork fox had found her Querencia ("The place of rest which the bull returns to, not noted for anything except the bull's preference for it"—Martha Graham) and had decided to stay.

So she remained to raise a family of four, and we continued to plant and cultivate our rows, skirting the nursery. Each time I approached the den on tractor I would veer off to north or south, so that gradually her home was buffered by a tufted oval patch of grass and weed. I question whether the fox family fully appreciated our sacrifice. It is much easier, and infinitely more efficient, to traverse a row and turn at the end. Out of respect we were obliged, on each tractor pass, while cultivating, to actually back out, reversing down the long row, occasionally nodding to the kits sunbathing near the entrance hole.

When the den is occupied the family seems content to keep to their little island; they have never damaged a crop of squash or spuds. And when the kits mature, they disappear. Now, because of an epidemic of mange, which has decimated the population of red fox, this choice habitation is left unoccupied. But I have made my yearly decision, influenced by the homing instinct of a succession of foxes. Against all rationale this spring we will skirt the fox hole once again, and extend an open invitation to our wild neighbors.

Home is a den, a burrow, a cave, a cottage, a nest, a treetop, a room, a penthouse, a pond, an ocean, a meadow, a set. On the final page of the last of his intricate literary works, James Joyce releases a cry: "Home!" In the classic children's story *The Wind in the Willows*, listen to Mole, at the end of a journey:

He stopped dead in his tracks, his nose searching hither and thither in its efforts to recapture the fine filament, the telegraphic current, that had so strongly moved him. A moment, and he had caught it again; and with it this time came recollection in fullest flood. Home!

When we speak of sense of place I imagine an invisible thread that connects the one who inhabits a place with a diversity of influences: soil, rock, water, weather, contact with other creatures. Within these influences a home is what is evoked when the invisible thread vibrates, like a steel string plucked by lost memory. We can listen for the particular pitch of the string and enter a story that defines a creature.

At the end of Love Lane, the dirt track that led to our cottage above the village of Mousehole, there lived an extended family of badgers. Although I never spotted a single one, and I looked often, the presence of these badgers was a dominant force, and they defined the place they chose for home. Love Lane crosses a narrow stream that meanders through the headland, and ends in the yard of a small farm. The fields that surround the stone cottage are bounded by granite walls, with several swinging gates. The farmer Tregenza pastured his cattle in the lush, wet fields; the grass was thick and nearly always wet, the bullocks moved from field to field through wide stone openings. For as long as we lived on the lane the farmer kept up a constant turf battle with the badgers. I was told that a family of badgers could claim a certain residence of their liking for over two hundred years; the place of their choosing is known as a set. No one I talked to had an exact count of the years this little civilization of badgers had existed. They were survivors.

Mr. Tregenza assumed the field was his; it was a perfect place to pasture his animals. But as the badgers continued to dig in, the grass surface became increasingly more treacherous for the cattle. The holes were scattered over a large area, creating a kind of green spongy moon surface. First the farmer attempted to fill the entrance holes with turf. This had no effect. Next he borrowed stones from the hedgerow and brought in rocks to plug the holes. Unbelievably, the badgers pushed the rocks to the side and tunneled elsewhere. Mr. Tregenza's despair was obvious, it hung in the air. He progressed to heavier rock, with no luck.

We often crossed this field on our way to a nearby village, so we watched the quiet drama unfold. The farmer, who rarely spoke, could be seen traveling on the lane with his van laden for his next vain attempt. One morning, as I climbed into the field over the iron gate, I noticed the bullocks at pasture within. But the field was diminished, and I caught the reflection of a new stretch of barbed wire fence. The battle was over for now. Farmer Tregenza had fenced the badgers in, to keep the bullocks out. The fence, of course, had no effect on the badgers' freedom of movement; it was simply that their set had, grudgingly, received the sanction of the man who "owned" it.

Returning on the lane to my dwelling I contemplated the meaning of home. I could name the abstract concepts of persistence and endurance to characterize the badgers' behavior, but the essence of animal community with the earth is beyond that. After a night of exploration, the badgers returned to the security of their underground tunnels, homing for the one exact spot on the headland they had chosen. When wind vibrates the Aeolian harp, the melody, an enchantment of mineral and air, can be heard in a field, in a set, a nest, a den, a cave, a cottage. Home is the invisible string, singing.

"SMILE, FOR YOUR LOVER COMES"

W alt Whitman knew how to be intimate with the soil and bedrock of Long Island:

> Smile O Voluptuous cool-breath'd earth. . . .
> Far swooping elbow'd earth—rich apple-blossom'd earth!
> Smile, for your lover comes.

This is an intimacy not often admitted by gardeners or farmers, except in the communicative solitude presented by a morning sea mist, or the illuminating, gentle fall of a spring night. The good gray poet, living in a more pastoral time, also wrote of "the music of the tin or copper bells clanking far or near," of the "milch cows" that he encountered while walking the farm lanes of Paumanock (the Native American name he chose to use for the island), "the south side meadows covered with salt hay."

The soil we are blessed with on Long Island, the "fat black earth," was deposited 21,000 years ago by the Wisconsinian glacier. The best of it, Bridgehampton loam, is a fine, sometimes heavy silt loam rich in mineral sediments from the outwash, able to support magnificent beech trees, hickory, cedar, and, at one time, the walnut. Cared for, this local loam will be rich in organic matter, easy to work—there are few pebbles, and fewer stones—and, though porous in places, it can also hold some water. We are blessed, too, with a long growing season; I have planted peas in the field in March, and harvested cabbage, for winter root cellaring, on December 28.

Our fields at Quail Hill are carpeted with many edible plants, both indigenous and introduced, forage food that was once commonly known (and ingested). To name a few—lamb's-quarters, purslane (which now sells for up to $18 per pound in New York's gourmet markets), curly dock, clover, and chickweed. When we seed spinach in April, we are sure to have lamb's-quarters (wild spinach) also germinate in the same soil. In the interest of maintaining clean fields I continue to encourage members of our farm to harvest these wild varietals.

Sagaponack—"place of the groundnut"—is a neighboring hamlet that derives its name from a plant indigenous to our soils, the demon weed nutsedge. To confuse all of us, there is another nut that frolics in our soil, and which also inspires a place name—Accabonac, a nearby harbor. Under the heading "groundnut," the yearbook publication of the Seed Savers Exchange has several listings of seed sources for this "sort of" potato, *Apios americana*. It is actually a wild leguminous vine—beware, snapdragons, cosmos, and statice!—that bears starchy tubers with an earthy, potato taste. A fellow gardener, who cultivates flowers on the Amagansett land where we raise vegetables, hoping to provide some root and air space for his flower seedlings, last year collected six fifty-gallon garbage cans of *Apios americana*, all from one acre. I have to admit I have some fear of this plant, and of that other nut (sedge) native to our soil. Nutsedge, or nut grass, can reproduce via the nut that lodges several inches down in the soil, and also by the headdress of seeds sprouting from the tough stalk. I suppose we should refer to these plants as heirlooms, though the meaning of that word is ever-evolving.

Heirloom, used properly, is actually the name chosen to define nonhybrid seeds introduced prior to 1940. Given the history of seeds and of man as an agriculturist, this seems a rather arbitrary date. Diversity, I know, has become a catchword, but a word we must repeat, I believe, like a chant. Where did our ancestors, or the Native Americans, or the later settlers of the Northeast get their seed? Seed was saved, carried, shipped, traded, let to reseed, saved again. All of this traffic ensured a diverse seed bank, one not calculated solely to produce the maximum weight at harvest. Two hundred years later, in respect to seeds, we have severely limited ourselves. Here is a quick list—since 1903, on a national level, we have lost 95 percent of our cabbage varieties, 94 percent of cucumbers, 89 percent of melons, 81 percent of tomatoes, 93 percent of lettuce varieties, and 96 percent of sweet corn. Such a list is discouraging; now is the time to diversify, and to encourage the vision of the Seed Savers Exchange: "When people grow and save seeds, they join an ancient tradition as stewards, nurturing our diverse, fragile genetic and cultural heritage."

The coastal Algonkians grew beans, squash, and corn, the three sisters, which could also be preserved for winter use in a porridge known as samp. A few years ago, when we assisted Lamont Smith from the Shinnicock nation in the re-creation of an Indian garden, I observed him practice an ancient planting method. In individual mounds he first placed a whole fish, an alewife, which he followed with corn seed, still very early in spring. Lamont timed the planting of the first corn by the run of the alewife in a local stream. The seeds were placed one, two, three, four, just above the buried fish, marking the four directions. As the corn grew, roots drank nutrients from the composting fish, and the four stalks supported one another, facing the north, south, east, west. When the ear of corn matured, the imprint of local water, wind, and soil filled the kernels.

Early farmers of the East End also used the sea's bounty for fertilizer, spreading menhaden, an oily fish, to feed the fields. We now use gallons of fish emulsion, which we buy in buckets from Neptune's Harvest, to feed nutrients to our seedlings before planting in the field. Fishing and farming have always been married in the folk wisdom of the South Fork: "When the lilacs arrive, so will the bluefish . . . an abundance of bass follows, with the white flowers of potato plants."

General Washington, when he toured Long Island late in the eighteenth century, expressed some anxiety concerning the farming practices he witnessed. He noted no use of rotations, essential to a sustainable agriculture, and little use of manuring, or composting. He was observing with the eye of a gentleman trained in field husbandry. Listen to the general's sympathy for economy with the natural world: "Orchard Grass of all others is in my opinion the best mixture with clover, it blooms precisely at the same time, rises quick again after cutting, stands thick, yields well and both cattle and horses are fond of it in green or in hay." George might have been pleased to witness the rotational practice and composting that we have used to revive our soil.

When we began farming here the soil was sad and lifeless, reduced to a medium for growing cash crops. For certification purposes, and for our own knowledge, we took samples to calculate the pH levels, and to record the overall health of the soil. In places the reading for "organic matter" was 1.7. Let me translate.

A reading this low, especially in ground classified as "prime agricultural soil," indicates that the soil has been exhausted; it is in need of some loving care. With such a reading, limited crops will have a chance to succeed; all plant life will almost surely be susceptible to disease or infection. In response we have fed the soil with compost, leaves and mulch straw, oats, rye, bellbeans and clover, field peas, and millet.

Fifteen years later we have increased the organic matter within our soils to 4.5 and over 5.0 in some places. This is impressive as a measurement of organic practice, but I am more interested in tangible reality; the kale is effervescent with leaves, tomato plants are long-lived and full of fruit, oats and rye mature evenly to a crisp and deep green. Because each crop has very specific needs, we work to increase the overall health of the soil, and then we "mix it up."

Roots, potatoes, vine crops, alliums, and brassicas will not be seeded or transplanted into the same ground for at least four years. I am satisfied with the health of the plants under such a rotation; for those who sample the fruits and leaves, taste is the relevant factor. In conversation and by survey, our farm members and chefs overwhelmingly encourage our ecological practices.

I love a knowledge so familiar with the ordinary as to invoke a word like "barleycorn." Here is Walt again: "In all people I see myself, none more and not one a barleycorn less. . . ." As we tend plants and soil, the perceived distances of time are often erased. I've just returned from the afternoon watering of thirty thousand young leeks and onions in the greenhouse. The wet "cool-breath'd earth," the gift of vast movement and change, contains nutrients of the past and present. Feeding the soil, and tilling, we are part of the seasonal and yearly round, turning over both seeds and the "word-hoarde" (Seamus Heaney's term) buried and shining in fertile soil. Hesitant to give advice, I offer some for open-minded apprentices and fellow gardeners: turn your spade into local loam, sand, silt, or clay, and witness the smile.

BEHOLD THIS COMPOST!

A poem by Keats, "To Autumn," has replaced the original stanzas that framed the farm members' map of Quail Hill Farm. That honor first belonged to an obscure poem, "This Compost," by Walt Whitman, discovered by our mapmaker Tim Laird. Excepting connoisseurs of Whitman, those who know this poem probably first read it printed on our farm map. Our Quail Hill T-shirt (an entrepreneurial inevitability)—designed by farm member Sarabelle Prince, which features carrots, lettuce, sugar snaps, hens, bees, a flying apple pie, and three scraggly farmers lazing in a field—also includes the first line of Walt's poem: "Behold this compost, behold it well!"

And we do behold it well, although our approach is perhaps less formal in practice than a recitation of Whitman's opening line. The word is returning to common usage thanks to a new generation of organic farmers and gardeners attentive to the spadework of a few agricultural pioneers. A class of fifth graders, when questioned, will all raise their hands to explain the meaning or describe Grandma's kitchen compost, at least in this community. When I give a tour of the farm, and we arrive at the compost heap, invariably I describe this as the true beginning, the place where soil fertility starts. "Behold it well!" Walt counsels.

For millennia gardeners and farmers across the Earth have used compost to feed the soil and the successive generations of plants. To compost is to build, replace, recycle, renew, energize. The word derives from Latin, *compositum,* meaning "to mix or blend," and refers to the combining of organic materials in order to create humus. Humus is the end product of plant and animal decomposition under favorable biological conditions. If we want health in the soil, if we want to produce plants or fruit, we want to encourage the formation of humus (lots of it).

My first close encounters with composting occurred on the steep cliffs of Penwith. There was a ritualistic element involved in Edgar's words and demeanor whenever the subject came up. He would usually prepare me months in advance—so I could contemplate the matter decomposing?—before we actually made the journey to the chosen farmyard where the choicest of materials had been aging, ripening to perfection.

Edgar: "I've gone up to look at 'im in the yard at Raginnis—'e's got the best manure I've seen around. We'll wait a fortnight, then go with some sacks and your Mini and fill up enough for we two."

I drove the Mini station wagon and Edgar carried the sacks. We bumped into the farmyard, searching for gardeners' gold; there it was, broken down, wet, heavy, teeming with worms and insects. Edgar's satisfaction was visible in his every gesture. He held the sack, I shoveled, the Mini sank with the weight; we arrived at the meadows as the sky darkened over the bay water. We stacked the sacks in an upper meadow, hidden behind the hedgerow, shadow men storing the gold. The magic of the moment had to do with very tangible matter, and with the elements within it and those elements that surrounded us in the mist on the cliffs.

Early in the twentieth century, Sir Albert Howard, who had studied botany at the Royal College of Science, conducted years of research in India, for which he is recognized as one of the founders of biological farming, and a pioneer of organic agriculture, originator of the Indore Compost Making Process. He was influenced by Franklin H. King's *Farmers of Forty Centuries,* written in 1911.

Howard's priorities were clear—he referred to nature as "the supreme farmer." By detailed experiment he proved that proper composting creates soil health, and that a healthy soil can create healthy plants with increased disease resistance. Sir Albert detailed the importance of mycorrhizae (mi-cor-i-zee), fungi found in good soil, but often absent in soil treated with synthetic chemicals. Abundant in humus-rich soils, mycorrhizae enrich plant roots through a symbiotic relationship, and their protein bodies are then absorbed by the plant. He stressed the need to compost, to return organic materials back to the soil in order to create humus, and to participate in "the great wheel of nature."

J. I. Rodale, a New Yorker, discovered Howard's *An Agricultural Testament* in 1941, and, energized by Sir Albert's ideas and research, he bought sixty acres of land in Emmaus, Pennsylvania, and launched his own magazine, *Organic Farming and Gardening*, to spread the word, in the following year. "Back to Nature in Agriculture" was printed on the cover of the first edition, which featured an introduction to organic farming by Rodale himself; an article on the Indore method of composting by Sir Albert and Dr. Ehrenfreid Pfeiffer introducing the biodynamic techniques; and Charles Darwin's piece "Vegetable Mold and Earthworms." Rodale brought out an edition of Howard's text, as well as issuing the influential work of Lady Eve Balfour, *The Living Soil*. The Rodale Institute has long been one of the lifelines for sustainable farmers in this country. Here is Sir Albert Howard, in *The Soil and Health*, inspired by his subject:

> To retrace our steps is not really difficult if once we set our minds to the problem. We have to bear in mind Nature's dictates, and we must conform to her imperial demand: (a) for the return of all wastes to the land; (b) for the mixture of the animal and vegetable existence; (c) for the maintaining of an adequate reserve system of

feeding the plant, i.e., we must not interrupt the mycor-
rhizal association. If we are willing so far to conform to
natural law, we shall rapidly reap our reward not only
in a flourishing agriculture, but in the immense asset of
an abounding health in ourselves and in our children's
children.

His commentary is sensible and succinct, mindful of the soil in
relation to social justice.

We were fortunate, when we began Quail Hill Farm, to discover
the owners of horse stables as some of our nearest neighbors. They
needed to find a home for the mounting piles of manure, and we
offered to provide the home. Once you have mastered a few of
the basic details involved with the composting process, the real
dilemma, which may appear simple on the surface, begins. How
to move the material—manure, food scraps, leaves and brush—
efficiently (please underline) from point A to point B. We failed mis-
erably in our first few years, to the chagrin of Wickitty Hotchkiss,
owner of Stony Hill Stables, due to the irregular performance of
our 1967 Dodge dump truck. Point A, adjacent to the riding school
ring, was often landscaped with mounds of manure until we could
nudge the Dodge back into transport mode. Add to this that a single
neighbor—a school custodian fearful of rodents, a town code offi-
cer, or a meticulous landscape gardener unused to viewing heaps of
decomposition—stationed midway between A and B can easily halt
the entire noble procedure.

If you are also fortunate, as we are, to own a back field that abuts
the railroad tracks and the county drainage sump, a place where
materials may compost undetected, and that your transport vehicle
is of a recent vintage, then you are free to turn your attention to the
recipe. Will Brinton, who operates Wood's End Lab in Maine, and
who has been called the Julia Child of composting, is the executive
chef of the business. When we applied for, and received, a SARE

(Sustainable Agriculture Research and Education, a rare, invaluable wing of the USDA) grant for a project entitled "Community Composting," we asked Will to act as consultant. He has served in a similar capacity on many other projects, including the organic farming operation backed by Prince Charles. At one point in the 1990s he was responsible for composting five to six tons of material per day in New York City, predominantly recycled kitchen scraps, through the use of a nifty composting bag that he designed and had manufactured. He has composted almost everything, from nitrate-laden farm wastes to hazardous explosives. His capabilities with compost—keep an open mind, now—heat up to the level of art or magic.

Our fields continue to improve because of Will Brinton's attention. Because our compost received a good grade, Will convinced us to make our own seed-starting mix, using our compost as a base, a practice we have honed to a rough (organic) science over the years. We sift and combine batch after batch of this seed-starting mixture, much as a baker mixes dough, to serve as a growing medium for thousands of transplants.

The ideal compost heap should contain a carbon/nitrogen ratio of 25:1 or 30:1. Too much carbon substance and the materials will not break down; an excess of nitrogen, and the mixture will burn too hot. Because the choice of bedding used by horse stables is wood chips, rather than straw, we are constantly in need of more nitrogenous material. I have offered to pay the difference between straw as bedding, and the cost of woody material, but my request is always declined. Wood chips act more efficiently to mask odor.

I find that wood chips, unfortunately, take at least a year and a half to break down sufficiently in order to be applied to the growing beds. Straw is a different matter. Even when applied as a mulch, straw will incorporate, usually within a season, after having provided a crust to discourage weed growth.

Compost that contains woody material, or any dense carbon substances, even in a "stable" condition, may, if applied to field or garden, actually rob plant life of nutrients. We hope instead, of course, to increase the capacity of the soil to impart nutrients to plants. This is an essential point. Manure is manure. Compost is the beneficial by-product of decomposition—raw materials are combined, and turned or aerated to facilitate a deconstruction process. Organic matter still in the process of breaking down actually requires energy from a soil medium. Finished, effective compost, similar to a well-prepared meal, supplies energy.

Until our recent association with the local, alternative Ross School, our finished compost was somehow lacking in color and flavor (too much carbon). Ann Cooper, author of *Bitter Harvest* and former executive chef, and until recently the head of the Center for Well Being at the school (she calls herself "the lunch lady"), is dedicated to recycling and composting. All of the Ross School students and faculty, who are served regional, organic, seasonal, sustainable (ROSS) food daily, are required to empty their plates into bins, and the leftovers from one thousand daily meals are then transported to our farm. Twice a week the school delivers a truck full of these food scraps, which we immediately incorporate into our compost windrows. So here is the nitrogen supply we had been missing, and we are also part of a living environmental science project. Due to our partnership with the school many students have seeded or transplanted leeks, tomatoes, or eggplant at Quail Hill, which they later taste as part of a Ross lunch. The taste is improved by the quality of the compost, which improves the quality of the soil, which in turn is improved by the recycling of leeks, tomatoes, or eggplant after lunch at Ross.

Perhaps the most frequently asked question relating to composting is: What can I throw into the heap? All things green is a good starting point, though matter of almost any color yearns to be included. Beware of oranges, however; citrus skins linger for a long time. A backyard gardener may safely include vegetable waste, grass clippings, assorted paper products (be attentive to the ink used), dry leaves, some sawdust, ash, and woody yard materials. He or she might want to avoid meat, bones, and weeds with seeds. Maintaining the correct carbon/nitrogen ratio ensures that the magic potion will act properly. Paper, for instance, has a ratio of 200/1, young grass a 15/1 ratio. A bale of straw stored next to the compost pile and littered between layers of food scraps will assist in aeration and will facilitate the decomposition. It is necessary to turn the pile, even if on an irregular basis, to ensure aerobic activity. Depending on the size of the heap, the instrument may be a fork, a bucket loader, or a state-of-the-art compost turner. Too wet and compact, and the microbes cannot do their work; too dry, and decomposition stalls.

"The bean bursts noiselessly through the mould in the garden . . . ," Whitman writes, and the gardener, bending near, pauses to check the process of humus formation. A liberal dressing of compost each year ensures this process, and the buildup of soil fertility. I prefer to spread the material in the autumn, which allows time for incorporation before spring planting, but, inevitably, spreading compost is also an April activity. We try to add ten to fifteen tons of finished compost per acre, every year, wherever we grow vegetables.

"The delicate spear of the onion pierces upward . . . ," Walt writes, until the plant matures and is harvested, and is lost to the field. Will Brinton estimates that 25 percent of the vegetable material that a farm produces actually leaves the field through harvest. What a loss! (Though I acknowledge that we have an obligation to feed people.) Therefore, the organic farmer must build a supply of organic matter to feed the field, to rebuild soil. For several years running, when we conducted our community-supported composting project, we estimated that we returned twelve to fifteen tons of vegetable matter to the Quail Hill fields. Farm members were given compostable food-scrap bags to fill with that part of the harvest they did not consume, and the bags went directly into our compost windrows. Within a month, if the piles were really cooking, the "food cycler" bags, lined with cellulose and packed with home-grown crop waste, were gone, thanks to a host of microorganisms.

Materials within a compost pile continue to break down until all the nutrients are enjoyed by resident organisms, though the process is really never-ending. Microorganisms—actinomycetes, fungi, and bacteria—arrive to assist the process, uninvited. When the pile is fresh, seemingly out of nowhere earthworms arrive by the thousands to participate. Earthworms aid in the formation of humus by leaving behind castings that Sir Albert calls "enriched earth." Continuous consumption by all of these tiny creatures can actually reduce the volume of compostable material by over one half. Perhaps this is what causes Whitman to exclaim, "How can you be alive you growths of spring?"

When the gardener or farmer begins to pile leaves, branches, grasses, peels, and petals, he or she is likely to acknowledge the food cycle as the great circle it really is—seed to soil to sprout to plant to fruit to harvest to consumption to compost to soil again. Walking through the valley in spring I see the full bouquet beginning to green up—vetch twining in the rye, the first buckwheat reappearing, red clover coming back, all improved by years of compost. With such lush growth the simple grasses and legumes feed the earth as well as the one who sows. The good gray poet commends the earth: "It gives such divine materials to men, and accepts such leavings from them at last."

"SURPRISED BY JOY, IMPATIENT AS THE WIND"

It is late May and my mind is full of blossoms, as days and weeks alternate with rain, rain, rain, then dry, dry, dry, then rain, rain. Today I looked closely, as if for the first time, on the hillock in front of our farm shop, after strong wind and a spring shower, at the various white—tinged with red—petals of dogwood, heart-shaped ornaments on a blanket of oak leaves. I had returned from a far field after mowing with the tractor, myself and mower deck covered with the aromatic flowers of Russian olive. Cropping the grass, I leaned into the hedgerow, into the late spring perfume, and as the tractor brushed branches, I was covered with a rain of blossoms. Later, descending the path to greenhouses and chickens, I was awakened to the wild by a single blossom of woodland geranium, cranesbill, from among a tangle of vines and my own thought.

Cranesbill, a herbaceous plant with beautiful lavender-pink flowers, has a particular fondness for the wooded hillside behind our farm shop. Several years ago, determined to discourage the spread of invasive brambles, I backed the tractor up the hillside and mowed down the thick brush. Cranesbill, responding to increased light, sprang up the following spring, clouds of flowers in the understory. Because this plant comes to blossom before the predominant oak trees and beech put out their leaves, a successful flowering is assured. When the invasive thorny and vine plants begin to dominate, I will again arrive to rescue this delicate woodland candle of late spring.

I have learned the meaning of the term "invasive" through observation of the rapid spread of Russian olive in one of our fields. This bush was once restricted to the no-man's-land that borders the railroad tracks, where it serves as an effective buffer, but over the course of only a few years small olives have cropped up here and there, in pockets of the field neglected by the mower blade. I have always supported, and sometimes encouraged, diversity within a field, but this ambitious woody plant, given the chance, intends to dominate a landscape. In spring the shiny silver leaves of Russian olive arrive early, and I have watched songbirds seek the shelter of the olive thicket. I admire the long, curving reach of branches, which sprout out of the central trunk. I also know others, alarmed by its rampant growth, who see this plant simply as an uninvited guest, rude and common by nature. But for this one moment in May, my shoulders dusted with the sweet-scented flowers, I choose to ignore the bad manners of an invasive. The perfume is intoxicating.

Walking under the beech canopy, through our stand of American hollies, I heard the greeting call of the eastern quail, at the foot of the hill that bears her name. Like myself, and our other farm workers, who may be kneeling among raspberry canes or hoeing in the trellised aisles of peas, the quail can be difficult to find. She is a small roundish bird, a ground dweller, and the color of her feathers mingles with the grasses. Once I was lucky—stepping through a weedy field I surprised a mother with four or five young, and I followed at a run as they scampered under twisting vines and matted grasses. It is rare at Quail Hill Farm, oddly, to actually see the bird. But if one is content to return her call of "bob-white, bob-white," and to wait for an answer from somewhere in the grasses, then a communication is established. I advise our farm members, who often search for us in field or orchard without success, to imitate the call of the quail. One of us, gardener or gamebird, will answer.

At this time of year the chicks, which we ordered in March, are nearing a teenage stage. They are active, anxious, and gangly. Each spring we hope to invigorate our flock of laying hens by introducing

a new covey of chicks. I leaf through the Murray McMurray catalogue with my children, who delight in the variety. I am drawn to
Buff Orpingtons, who have proved to be the most persistent set-
ters and mothers; Black Giants for their size and grace; Speckled
Sussex for their plumage; Anaconas, the rainbow layers, for their
blue-green eggs. My children select the smaller birds, who strut and
peck with a recognizable dignity: black-tailed buff Japanese, Silver-
Spangled Hamburgs, and the comic Polish varieties, which are listed
as the "top hat specials."

When the chicks arrive by overnight mail, packed in a perfo-
rated cardboard box, we receive our yearly summons from the
Amagansett postal clerk: "Your package has arrived, and the peep-
ing is driving us crazy!" The tiny laying hens are kept alive—when
they are shipped in the cold—by
the inclusion of a number of
roosters of unknown variety,
employed to provide some
warmth. I was amazed to
discover, after receiving
our first box of chicks,
that those of lesser intelligence must be taught how
to drink. My experience in
handling babies was invaluable.
A farmer, usually adept at fitting and mending tractor implements
and pounding stakes, must also learn how to hold a fuzzy head the
size of a thimble and to dip a tiny beak into water. I cannot be sure,
but following the course of instruction I believe I have sensed gratitude in the bearing of certain Buff Orpingtons.

The spring is cold, so plant growth is slow. Because our weather
is determined by the water—we are surrounded by it on all sides—
until the ocean temperature begins to rise, we continue to shiver.
And so do most of the young plants. But for a week or two longer,
in the shadow of beech and holly, wild geraniums, columbine, and

sweet rocket sparkle in the woods. The perennial herbs—oregano, thyme, chives, lemon balm, and mint—are filling out in the round herb garden. Rhubarb sprouts new stalks daily, and asparagus shoots up through the mulch. Red mustard, broccoli rabe, and the Oriental greens—mizuna, toriziroh, and tatsoi—favor this time of year.

"Surprised by joy, impatient as the wind" (Wordsworth), I am quietly amazed to still be tending these particular fields, years after first pushing a wheel hoe through this loam. Traditional field husbandry accompanies husbandry at home, and fatherhood. Staying late to finish another field I am caught by the frenzy of spring. At Quail Hill I prepare the ground for a succession of annual crops. When I return home and open the door I am engaged in a perennial cycle—raising kids. Tending and serving both plants and people are, to put it mildly, humbling experiences. When I read at night to my child, the words rise to take shape in air just as a tender stem rises from a seed placed in soil. The changes I witness daily—in both plants and children—are delicate and cumulative. As a father and farmer I search for the wellspring of patience, and I know the value of a good listening ear.

Entangled with the task of sorting out details and mishaps this spring, perhaps I have been neglectful of the seasonal changes slowly unfolding. Marybeth S., a founding member of our farm, reminded me yesterday of the original impetus that led to our revival of community farming. She recalled a day at the farm with her young nephew, harvesting fingerling potatoes for the first time. Reaching into the soil, from the plant that rose out of a single seed potato, they uncovered innumerable spuds held together on the root network, delicate and substantial. Held in the air and reversed, this simple starch, she said, was a symbol for the tree of life.

Years ago, when we lived in a studio on the Cornish hillside, the mahogany desk I had built was covered with seeds, scraps, petals, small sculptures, and gifts of art, much like my fold-up table above the Quail Hill shop. There I would write, or try to, most mornings, gazing out at the dark Cornish sky and the fulmar gulls returning to nest in cliff pockets above the bay, under a ledge of granite. Less and less I met with the illusive, difficult words of discourse, more and more with simple words like stone, field, rose, shore. Slowing down this spring I find on my desk: rock, nest, everlasting. And above, inscribed with his pen, a two-line poem entitled "Reefs," by my former teacher Milt Kessler: "The mind must/ love the heart." Ah, look, another blossom!

SUMMER

Every leaf shakes the light again,
begins to talk . . .

Cicadas
have found
their August voice.

Surprisingly lightly
everyone lets go:
ripe now, all we've
sung into being
since before the leaves. . . .

—MEGAN CHASKEY,
"AUGUST," 1994

A LOAD OF HAY, A SILVER SPOON

With a beekeeper's quietude he slips into the valley to attend our four hives of honeybees whenever there is a need. We may not be aware of his visits, the bees certainly are. When the frames within the supers are full of honey, Tony, having prepared another box of frames complete with wax foundations, sets another super on top, giving the workers space to move, and space to store more food. Starting in early spring, Tony is at work in and around our farm shop, cleaning boxes and frames, fixing the wax foundation to frames, leveling the sites near the orchard for each hive. Because of the destructive varroa mite—which, alarmingly, has devastated perhaps 80 percent of the wild bees in this country, and an equal share of managed hives—we have had to replace our hives nearly every spring for several years running. Tony travels to upstate New York, and returns with new queens and colonies. We set them up in their new lodgings, and pray to our distant sun. Worker bees are happy throughout a season blessed with sun—flowers mature over a long period of time, pollen will be plentiful, and every day is a working day. In a wet year, however, bees are forced to remain in the hive, unable to gather the dust of flowers, and their need to build a store for winter is frustrated by the fickle weather. According to Tony, our bees have made good use of our helping of bright days.

To keep the Quail Hill bees working into the autumn, we sow buckwheat wherever we can. A member of the Polygonaceae family, buckwheat grows quickly, and comes to flower in just thirty days. Bees and other pollinators adore the white blossoms, which supply pollen for a delicious dark, hearty honey.

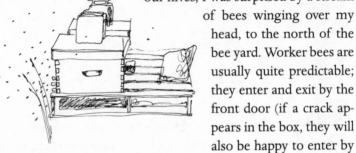

Earlier this spring, while observing our hives, I was surprised by a stream of bees winging over my head, to the north of the bee yard. Worker bees are usually quite predictable; they enter and exit by the front door (if a crack appears in the box, they will also be happy to enter by a side door, or a back door). As my eye followed the flight of a single bee—ah, look, in the wild cherry, a swarm!—it was my luck to be in the right spot to discover a recent exodus, by the queen and her attendants, and a crowd of workers, from one of our hives. They were parked for a short time, fastened to a small branch, a mere three feet from the ground as scouts searched surrounding forest and field for a more proper home. A portion of the population of an active hive may choose to swarm, to follow the queen and abandon the present home, for any number of reasons. Douglas Whynott describes swarming as "a form of group reproduction, or colony division, like a cell dividing." When bees depart they collect on a nearby branch or sapling or sunflower stem, where they build a little temporary cosmos around the queen.

The first swarm I "rescued" (the terminology reflects a certain hubris) was rather precariously balanced on a tangle of grasses that was precariously balanced on a windy rock headland above Mount's Bay, Cornwall. The bees nearly leapt into the cardboard box I held beneath them. Likewise, this swarm, a triangular mass half hidden in the small wild cherry, was a gift to a beekeeper. I called Tony immediately, and he was at the scene within minutes (good speed for an eighty-year-old). It is wise to act with speed—the scout workers are eager to bring to their queen news of a choice new home. When she receives such news there is no delay—off they go to construct the new hive in the chosen habitat.

We readied a box, complete with ten frames fitted with wax foundations, and slid the box under the branch heavy with bees; then Tony unceremoniously shook the cherry tree. A triangular fist of bees landed with emphasis on the frames, and the air was a cyclone of flying insect bodies. Yet, within minutes most of the swarm was inching down the wax forms into its new abode.

The success of such an escapade is based entirely on one's ability to persuade the queen. Wherever she decides to go, even if she is shaken there, all others will follow. Ten minutes after our act of persuasion, we placed our new hive adjacent to the existent working hives, on pallets raised slightly off the ground, facing a wild patch of orchard grass and small cedars. I still think of this as curious; one of our original colonies, with unsolicited, chance assistance, found a new home just a few feet to the east of an almost identical home it had chosen to abandon an hour earlier. Perhaps we should reflect—could restless *Homo sapiens* discover some advantage in this innovative method of house hunting?

It is good fortune to witness any swarm from an existing hive, but this spring I had the luck to happen upon a total of four swarming colonies. We captured three, one with the help of our acrobatic field manager, Matt C. This batch of bees had bypassed the two adjacent wild cherries—chosen by swarms one and two—to settle out of reach on a swooping hickory branch. We approached the branch with our Case 495, a tractor fitted with a front-end bucket loader. Then we placed a box full of frames in the bucket, and raised it to just under the thick swarm. Matt climbed a ladder placed near the bucket loader, cut away some smaller branches, and, with authority, bounced the hickory branch above his head. Although the air was black and bristling with bees, this maneuver had to be repeated three times before the queen was dislodged from her temporary resting place. Given that she is surrounded by, say, twenty thousand bees, the chance of spotting her is unlikely. Even the most mellow of beekeepers can be rattled by such an event. Although swarming bees are extremely unlikely to sting, the insistent buzzing of swirling insects can jar anyone's nerves.

The final swarm of the year I encountered at the beginning of summer, the twenty-ninth of June, near enough to July to heed the words of the traditional rhyme:

> A swarm of bees in May
> Is worth a load of hay.
> A swarm of bees in June
> Is worth a silver spoon.
> A swarm of bees in July,
> Let the buggers fly!

Still, I followed them, these brief visitors to the Earth—workers live about six weeks—as they rained up into the sky before swirling and descending to a chosen branch of Russian olive. I waited to watch a few thousand begin to build a circle of motion around their queen, and then I turned to harvest carrots, and to let them fly.

"THE FAINTLY VISIBLE TRACES"

Hovering at my window the hummingbird was perhaps drawn to a color reflected in the glass. This was only my second encounter with a hummingbird at Quail Hill. The first came but a few weeks previous, and was shared by my son Liam, as we walked near the lower greenhouse. A pair of hummingbirds— iridescent, quick—were feeding high up in the American hollies. This led me to notice, for the first time, the abundance of delicate holly flowers, like small bells overflowing the deep green of *Ilex opaca*. Waking early one morning as we approached the summer solstice, I wrote:

> Under Ilex
> nectar's lure—
> clusters of holly
> flower in the breeze
> of hummingbird's wings.

Later in the day, while I was working at my desk in the farm shop, suddenly at my window (having heard?) the messenger hummingbird appeared. We faced each other through the glass, equally alert, though my wings were quiet.

In the middle of the summer season a chorus of thunder and water arrives again in north Amagansett. Zoe the farm cat seeks solace, and a torrent washes down the slope toward the hens, erasing our daily footprints. Most of the farm crew is gathered in the shop—cleaning, sorting, tying, and hanging the crop of garlic, to ensure proper drying. Our most appealing-looking variety this year is German White, with five or six large cloves, hot to the taste when fresh.

Our cabbages continue to grow to epic proportions; green, yellow, and purple beans flourish on Hurricane Hill. We are already tasting green peppers, to be followed by another nightshade, eggplant, and then fine, fat onions. When the "love apples" begin to ripen I look forward to an unusually large fruited paste tomato, affectionately named French Barnyard. Calista W., a farm member, found this varietal in a French garden. She borrowed a specimen, carried it home, saved the seed and shared it with us, and *Voilà!* an ordinary Gallic paste tomato debuts in Amagansett.

As we make our rounds to tend the plants on harvest days, we also take part in the conversational hum that is generated by harvesters in the field. Other community farmers, surprised that our cooperative members are willing to march out into the field and dig carrots or cut chard or pinch herbs, often ask, "But how do you get them to do that?"

I respond, with some pride: "This is part of the foundation of this particular community farm. The first families chose to dig in, literally, and yes, they enjoy it."

No system is perfect, of course. An apprentice recently overheard one member, burdened with bags of produce, call out to his wife, while deciding whether or not to take time to dig for potatoes: "They think we like to do this!"

At the same time, in another field, a new member obviously in love with the Quail Hill plant diversity quietly intoned to me, "We are still learning leaf." I thanked her for giving precise voice to a farmer's thoughts.

As I water the flats of vegetables nearly ready for transport to the fields, there they are—honeybees darting and resting on Ermosa, Red Sails, Waldmann's, and Plato II, our latest planting of lettuces. Having provided these bees with a new home in what our farm map labels as "The Bee Loud Glade" (thanks to W. B. Yeats and Sarah), we now provide them with liquid refreshment, daily, as we water the plants in and around the greenhouses in the valley. It is a welcome sight—honeybees hearty and hard at work in the summer. We provide a patch of wild valley, and an abundance of flowers and buckwheat to add to their natural cuisine. We add a dose of well water twice daily (as we water our seedlings). They delight us with their flight, their intricate community, and their communication with sweetness.

Our bees have made a recovery in this summer season, primarily due to Mary W., who now visits the hives in our valley. She speaks to them, quietly and continually, as she opens the supers to check on the queen's activity and the workers' industry. She is generally free of a suit or veil, choosing to meet them with a vulnerable self. The effectiveness of such human action is the subject of ancient sutras and scripture. In Mary's case I believe the motivation—and practice—is instinctual.

At a recent "Bee Talk," which took place at the Quail Hill bee yard, Mary created such an atmosphere of ease that children sat on her lap to view the workers whisking in and out of the hive entrances. The air was punctuated with bees in flight and people anxious to understand the dance. When she displayed a super full of honey the audience was sympathetic—men, women, and children were now guests of the bees, and several had to be persuaded to touch a finger to the waxen comb heavy with sweetness.

There is a harmony that is almost tangible in the fields at this time of year, and that arrives with the ripening of fruit on plants seeded in the greenhouse four months earlier. It is a predictable result of shared labor and appreciation for that labor, but I cannot describe the quality at the source—which is energetic, the by-product of plants respiring. I am reminded of a curious poem by Robert Frost, inscribed on a plaque facing a Vermont field beside the narrow Middlebury River: "We dance round in a ring and suppose / But the Secret sits in the middle and knows."

Nourished by plenty of water, the orange flower heads of *Asclepias* are brilliant against the browning grasses. The pond—which disappears during dry weather—has returned to flood the circle of

asters at the edge of Deep Lane. This year, in moments of rest, I hear water droplets sound in waves, the rain after a rain, pushed from leaves when wind disturbs the still woods. Down by the hollies, where I first saw a summer hummingbird, and here at my window in the woods, something of the whirr of her wings remains. Gary Snyder says, "The faintly visible traces of the world are to be trusted." Traces like the flute of a far-off warbler among the oaks (resembling a tin whistle in a cathedral), or the color of butterfly weed almost hidden in wild grasses, or the hazy, pervasive sound of bees feasting on the nectar of squash flowers, bergamot, oregano, thyme, and clover.

A SEAMLESS GARMENT

Orioles rasp by us at such speed through the valley that we see only a gold flash. By August that color will echo from the sunflowers sprouting along the front face of our farm. Each year we sow a few rows of sunflowers as a doorway into the vegetable garden. The varieties change, but Autumn Beauty, multicolored and branching, usually dominates the first row, facing Deep Lane and the morning sun. Selma Suns, Taigo, and Italian White share the space with Autumn Beauty, and the second tier belongs to Mammoth Gray Stripe and others of the strain *Uniflorus giganteus*.

How extraordinary that a small seed can sprout to a height of ten feet or more and produce an ornamental circular face decorated with a maze of seeds, weighing in at five pounds. Wasps, hover-flies, sparrows, bumblebees, gardeners—all admire the abundance of *Helianthus,* the sun circle of petals and seeds. In a birthday poem to my daughter I wrote:

> After rain helianthus
> leans to comb grass.
> A clown's face fades
> inwardly to precise seeds
> smiling: child, child . . .
>
> Blackbirds, catbird, and flicker
> dress the summer dusk with music.

Everyone who comes to the farm in late August will wade in among the sunflower stems, to cut branching flowers. Now, in June, I watch as thousands of plants fulfill their mission—to create an in-dividual stalk thick enough to hold a substantial weight of seeds. This year, at seeding time, in a moment of inspiration I reached into my bucket of seeds to find a packet of Crackerjack marigolds. I mixed the Crackerjacks with Autumn Beauty seeds, so now a deep green cloud of stems and leaves is laced along the row of sunflower stalks.

A short time ago, after the cold spring, the valley was bare; now when we look up we are surrounded by a leaf canopy, the interior of sky. The profusion of the wild and the cultivated becomes a seam-less garment.

Sailing into June, most of the early, first-season planting is done, so now we begin to share our garden with the natural abundance also known as weed. Many of these wild cultivars are of course edi-ble, such as the leaves of lamb's-quarters, happily at home in our fields, sometimes dwarfing the emerging carrots. And, as flowers begin to form on our seeded crops, we find garnishes everywhere, some that will add fine flavor to a salad. Soon we will harvest the flowers of nasturtium, borage, and the Oriental green hon-tsai-tai, whose flowers hold a hint of coconut. When arugula buds up, we are given another flavor to accompany the leaves. We try to provide continual plantings of greens, so that somewhere on the farm, with close inspection, members will find tender leaves. We encourage harvesters to thin the outside leaves of plants, thus stimulating new growth. If properly harvested, certain plants, such as Swiss chard, will stand and reproduce new leaves throughout three seasons. Conversely, if any plant is stripped of its leaf life, it will go into shock. I have seen a bare, treelike stalk of kale recover, but only if we can herd the harvesters in various other directions.

So we are content to share some of our garden with weeds, on a temporary basis, certainly not all of the garden, and we are less than polite to nut grass (nutsedge). I have heard various farmers quietly complain of a twenty-year battle with quack grass or couch grass. Nut grass claims this place of dishonor on Quail Hill Farm. I once read—and quickly tried to forget—that the USDA rates nutsedge as the number-one most noxious weed. Yow! I did not have contact with this spiky fellow before my move to Long Island, so I turned to several of the farm families with generations of experience. I recall a moment of frustration, after I had asked Larry H. of the Green Thumb, "Just what do I do about nut grass?"

His reply was quick, and concise: "Move your farm."

Faced with yet another profusion of nut grass I have considered this advice, but instead we stay with our chosen fields, and search for other options. At first we reached down to pull each spike after emergence, but we learned that this could easily become a full-time occupation. It is almost impossible to retrieve the nut—usually buried two to three inches deep—along with the roots and stem of sedge. Within a few weeks the ambitious nut has sent up another shoot, to crowd out any other seedlings. Even the sharpest hoe, handled by an experienced cultivator, will only cut the nut grass stalk, effectively adding strength to the root of the plant. And nut grass, similar to other weeds, tends to choose an area and to multiply, eventually maturing to a kind of carpet. An observer, unfamiliar with the habits of invasive weeds, would assume that such a carpet was intentionally planted.

As a part of our rotation system we consistently leave one field or another fallow for a year, usually seeded with a legume such as clover. The field is "at rest," after years of supporting crop after crop. But we have found that under the surface of the sod, undisturbed for a year, nut grass is definitely not at rest. When we turn the soil over the following spring, there it is, a full squadron of sedge, seemingly encouraged by our design to include a fallow in the rotation. So how do we make the correct ecological choice? Nut grass is resistant to our hands, our hoes, the shoes of the cultivating tractor, heavy mulches, and the cries of a frustrated farmer. One of our first apprentices, Rockwell, a dedicated man with a hoe, early one morning revealed a nightmare he could not shake off. There was no escape for him in the dream—as fast as he could run he could not outdistance the gigantic nut grass that pursued him. Although we offered sympathy, it was difficult for the remainder of the summer to send him into certain portions of the field.

What do you do with a plant that can easily penetrate potatoes? The spud is not harmed by the spike, nor by the nut lodged in starch, but children and chefs prefer potatoes—whether mashed, baked, or fried—sans a spear of grass.

David O., whose family has farmed in Wainscott, near Bridgehampton, for generations, offered some help: "They say that the nut forms after the fourth of July—if you can get to it before then, you've got a chance. And next year the ground will be cleaner. After the fourth the nut is formed—you've lost."

Following his advice we've discovered a method, designed to bring the nut to the surface, where it will actually dry out in the sun. After plowing we wait for the first flush of nut grass to appear. If the weather is dry we follow with a disc harrow to spread the nut out on the soil surface. In a few weeks, when the next flush of sedge appears, we disc again, and the sequence continues. By mid-July, and through a special arrangement with the summer sun, we've reduced the population of nutsedge, in one field, at least for a time. Now we follow this forced fallow with a seeding of late-season root crops or with transplants of autumn brassicas.

It is said that this illusive nut was considered a food by Native Americans. I've tasted it, and I choose to leave it for others, but my judgment is far from objective. Abby G., an apprentice, compared the taste to pine nuts, but I am quite certain that I could distinguish the difference when served with a nutsedge pesto over linguine. It is a determined, tenacious plant, a Taurus of the vegetative kingdom. Given freedom, nut grass will sprout a headdress of sharp seeds atop a very tough stalk. This is persistence in a plant—it can reproduce both by underground nut, and by aboveground seed. And still I cannot consider a weed as an enemy. But, eerily, I hear the voice of John Keats: "The sedge has withered from the lake / And no birds sing! . . ."

The peas are beginning to bloom; shucking peas are the first—Coral, Green Arrow, and the heirloom, Lincoln. The exquisite purple flowers of Sumo will follow, then sugar snaps, and prolific Mammoth Melting snow pea, climbing to seven feet high, above the trellis. As we glide into summer with the diving finches we see the green hem of the valley garment flash with the sea's light. Seamless—gold through green, finch through bramble, honeysuckle, and the wild grasses, seamless—through the quilted valley.

EQUANIMITY

The front cover of *Successful Small-Scale Farming: An Organic Approach*, by Karl Schwenke, displays a photograph of a seasoned farmer seated high up on a vintage Farmall (with a wide wheel base), his shoulders at ease, making his way on a fine day along a farm lane that ends in the sweet green of the back field. The brim of his cap is tipped up, as is his gaze; the field is newly mown, probably for hay, and his tractor is not fitted with any implement. In other words, he is out for a ride, or in transit from one task to another. Leafy branches from a stand of hardwoods reach out and over the contoured field.

The image is emotive; anyone who has farmed can share in the feeling of the easeful ride in the late afternoon. Although more often than not the farmer is motivated by a sense of urgency—or the opposite, a sense of relief—this man, riding out alone, has found some equanimity. He has worked hard for what we will call the freedom of the open field.

It is characteristic for the farmer, or gardener, to embrace solitude. Faced with the daily reality of earning a living, to find some solitude may be another matter. Although Edgar Wallis appeared willing to coax me into the Penwith meadows at every opportunity (always encourage a willing worker with a cliff shovel), I know he valued the meadows as I did, for the exquisite solitude to be found there. Alone in a small walled meadow one could hear the sound of waves rushing into stone far below, the calls and echoes of jackdaws

and gulls, the crisp voice of a passing cuckoo; and as the day drew to
a close, the colors of sea and sky merged to surround the gardener
with a sensuous blanket. In those meadows I learned the delicacy of
a loneliness shared with the world of plants. Breathe deeply and
communication commences.

Having retired my cliff shovel to become lead man with a hoe
for a community farm, I have had to sacrifice some vocational solitude. But I have gained companions in the field—many who have
come to recognize the value of a field worker's solitude. Returning
to a place, coming to know a place, one may experience land, in
Leopold's words, as "a community to which we belong."

Terry Tempest Williams writes the following, as part of her essay on the commencement address she gave at the University of
Utah, in the spring of 2004:

> Before the speech, I had the great pleasure of meet-
> ing with a group of graduating seniors. When I asked
> them what they felt we were most in need of as a society
> and nation, the answer was a unified one: building com-
> munity.

All of the literature that exists to encourage CSA farms includes
in the formula the formation of a responsible, solid, committed "core
group." These individuals—meeting in a working barn, an orchard,
or a room filled with bee equipment or tractor implements—are
those most inspired to build community. I happen to possess an
original copy of Robyn Van En's *Basic Formula to Create Community
Supported Agriculture*, a xeroxed text, copyright 1988, bound with a
bit of glue and a strip of blue duct tape (it still holds). This home-
spun treatise begins with an epigram from an inscription on a church
in Sussex, England, 1730:

> A vision without a task is but a dream, a task without a vision
> Is drudgery, a vision with a task is the hope of the world.

In the case of Quail Hill Farm it was a core group of ten families that actually planted the first seeds of the community farm. This group of people was the embodiment of the link between "producer and consumer" (that word "consumer" has an unfortunate echo; recently, at the suggestion of a progressive Danish farmer and thinker, Thomas Hartung, I was encouraged to substitute "citizen" for consumer). The group's role, similar to that of a board of directors, but predominantly advisory, changes with the seasonal fluctuations in the needs of the community. At a significant point in the growth of our farm, although as growers we had developed a successful farm production system, we were somewhat neglectful of the shareholders (the citizens). The core group—or farm committee—recognized the oversight and worked to support the production of community (to accompany the production of vegetables). In *Sharing the Harvest*, an invaluable guide to CSA farms, Liz Henderson quotes a core group member of Angelic Organics, a large CSA located outside of Chicago:

> The more we do as shareholders to help with non-farm tasks, the more our hearty and visionary farmers can concentrate on producing the delicious, colorful, nutritious, aromatic, and simply splendid veggies and fruits we have come to depend on from June to November.

Well, hearty and visionary farmers are just what we need to revive our agricultural economy; it follows that more than a single person who wields a hoe, or tractors down endless rows, is needed to work the earth. It requires a family, a tribe, a community that holds land in trust, a core of people in support of soil, to urge us toward sustainability in agriculture.

Late June, 6:30 AM, a misty morning in the orchard. Today is the first food event of the year, the annual farm breakfast, which brings hundreds of people to Quail Hill, some to learn what happens here, some in search of herbed eggs, raspberry pancakes, Jane's roasted potatoes, Gordian's onion tarts. The members do it all; my job is to ascend the soap box (apple crate, actually) for a ritualistic few minutes of speaking. After years of bungling this and that, we are now almost professional. Robert S. transports the grills from his nearby home, David D. skillfully keeps the coffee—and the electricity—coming to the orchard, Nick S. is everywhere with hammer and screw gun, Gordian R. is flipping pancakes with pizzazz.

Jane Weissman, who formerly directed Green Thumb, New York City's community gardening program, is the wizardess in charge of this event. A year ago we decided it was time to honor her years of service to the farm. A special edition of "Quail Hill Farm News" contained the following: "Weissman, the brains and muscle behind the ubiquitous organic farm journal was caught completely unaware of the fact that she had been selected by the International Community Supported Agriculture Subcommittee as this year's recipient of the Nobel Prize for Vegetable Reporting." A clairvoyant "agriprentice" described Jane as "so sweet that flea beetles like her." We are fortunate that she has a veteran community gardener's sense of humor.

Before the sun is high in the early summer sky, those who have broken bread and tasted herbs return to the fields to harvest radishes, rhubarb, butterhead and romaine, the first hakurei turnips. I'm off to another field to keep up with the seeding. We are fortunate, this year, for a clear day. My thoughts return to a different year, when we were learning to judge the weather of the South Fork, and the moods of community farm members. I wrote a letter, after the birth of my second son, ecstatic with a new life, testing the waters of another nascent partnership:

> I'm rocking with my infant son today, his sounds timing with rain on roof or deck, or with the rush of

thunderstorm through oaks. He's eleven days new, and I'm lulled with him halfway between two worlds; we're content to watch the storm's movement, his first witness of such exterior power, my wish answered for rain. On my first return visit to Quail Hill, I felt an ache and inadequacy, a farmer's despair for an uncompromising partner (Nature herself). Less than an inch of rain in two months is not enough to nourish plant life. Farm members this year will understand the basic agreement of CSA—members agree to share the risks of farming with the farmer. What we can do is to try to reduce the risks.

The farmers thank you for what we perceive as your understanding. For us, the agricultural ethic implies trust in the natural, naturally various order. We take care to care first for the soil and her fruits. Scarcity and abundance share equal measure in the cosmology. My son opens his eyes to the drum of rain, his quick kicks still timed to liquid, his nine month residence. I've seen it— birth requires great courage and patience, as does daily work, part of an infinite series.

Years later, toward the end of another harvest and community day, and the end of a week in June near to the summer solstice, I find myself in the far field seeding a potential second crop of roots—carrots and white turnips. Here in this open land, bounded by thick hedges on every side, I'm out of the sight of all save the red-tailed hawk, who prefers to roost at the top of the high tension towers that border the tracks. His relative, the sharp-shinned hawk, sails by, low over the field, searching for a movement in the grass. Crows cackle in the high branches of sassafras. The seeds click against the revolving seed plate before they slip down the metal chute to rest in soil. I am alone and in company with the music that seeds make and the feathered drift of raptors in the fertile solitude of the back field.

THE WOLF'S PEACH

It is with a touch of trepidation that I assume the responsibility to speak of the apple of paradise. Just a few years ago, a fellow farmer and myself, facing yet another year filled with hours and hours of nightshade duties, debated whether our Quail Hill Farm members would notice if we accidentally forgot to plant the tomatoes. In short, they would. Although we grow more than fifty crops (over 225 varieties), the favorites remain: lettuce, potatoes, onions, greens, tomatoes. Our reluctance on one particular year does not reflect distaste, only an honest hesitation to deal with the demands of thousands of nightshades also known as the "love apple." Given good soil, sun, and some water, it is easy enough to grow tomatoes; it is not easy to grow them well. Determined to improve our reputation, and respectful of the love apple's friendship with garlic and basil, we continue to experiment with *Lycopersicon* ("wolf's peach") *esculentum.*

The tomato is a member of the Solanaceae family, which also includes potatoes, peppers, eggplant, and tobacco. Native to South America, tomatoes probably originated in the coastal highlands of Peru and Ecuador. The wild form is also found in Mexico and Central America; ancient drawings tell us that Peruvian Indians cultivated the tomato as early as the fifth century BC. The Spanish encountered this plant in Mexico, sometime after 1519, and then carried seed to the Caribbean and the Philippines. Matthioli, an Italian herbalist, first mentions the "mala aurea" (golden apple) in 1544.

The first report of the tomato in North America was made by William Salmon, after 1680, and it may have arrived via the Caribbean. This new fruit was not an overnight success. Some complained of the odor of the plant, others feared the poisonous glycoalkaloids found in the leaves of other nightshades, and still others preferred to use this vine plant as an ornamental. Tomatoes were also grown for medicinal purposes; they are a good source of vitamin C and potassium. The love apple is also a major source of lycopene, a substance similar to beta-carotene, thus effective as an antioxidant.

At present, the annual United States tomato crop is valued at over one billion dollars; 80 percent of this crop is harvested mechanically for processing. Americans consume over twelve million tons of tomatoes each year. Most commercial varieties sold are hybrids, and there are a great many of these, but note the number of open pollinated varieties distributed by various seed saving groups. The Seed Savers Exchange yearbook contains about 125 pages of tomatoes, over three thousand varieties; the legendary Ben Quisenberry tested thousands on his own. Carolyn J. Male, who publishes a newsletter devoted entirely to heirloom tomatoes, keeps a data base that lists ten thousand USDA registered varieties. Dr. Carolyn, a beautiful pale yellow cherry tomato, named for this lover of the love apple, which produces fruit throughout the entire season, was a new favorite at the farm this year.

While discussing tomatoes we should clarify some terms. Hybrid plants are the product of two parent plants, chosen and developed by breeders in the interest of greater yields, uniform ripening, shipping quality, or disease resistance. Seed saved from hybrids will not breed true; the offspring will tend to revert to one of the original parents. The use of hybrids predominates in conventional agriculture. Open pollinated (OP) varieties are not overly manipulated by man, and they have been tested by time. Heirlooms are open pollinated varieties introduced before 1940. Open pollinated plants can perform better under adverse conditions, and they offer the possibility of something often sadly missing in hybrids—good taste! For the gardener wishing to save seed, OP varieties may serve as an introduction into the magical realm at the interior of the plant world.

Before the decision is made to order seeds, it is helpful to consider the labor required by determinate and indeterminate plants. Indeterminates are viney—they can grow to seven or eight feet. Determinates are bush shaped, so they will require less staking, or none, depending on your need to establish order. We have tried most staking methods known to man, accompanied by vile language and disaster, but in the end we have settled on three basic techniques. We have patented a rather hilarious procedure, needing several farmhands and a few monkeys, once the peas elsewhere in the garden are exhausted. We cut away the pea vines, place a person at each stake, and walk the snaking trellis over to the tomato patch, to be used once again, this time as support for the very viney cherry tomatoes. Cherries are often the first to ripen, and the last to be picked, and as such are indispensable in the garden. Perhaps unfairly, Sungold, a cherry, tends to win our Tomato Tasting year after year. My favorite is Matt's Wild Cherry, a little sweet red one that often ripens an entire cluster at once. The tiny White Currant is in fact too sweet for some palates, though children are drawn to its candy quality.

Another staking technique, claimed by multiple states (the New Jersey weave, the Florida weave, the Texas weave), remains the method of choice, especially if you are providing for many harvesters. Stakes, one to two inches thick, are pounded in along the row, at intervals of about ten feet, two to three plants between each stake. Then, using twine or baling string, the gardener weaves in and out of the stakes and plants, up and back along the row. As the plants mature, another weave is added, before the vines leap or fall to the ground. Depending on the commitment of the weaver, the strength of the twine, the relative humidity, and the willingness of the tomato plant, the results of this substantial effort tend to vary widely, to say the least. Ultimately, this method allows for increased air circulation, and gives the fruit a place to ripen just a little nearer to the sun.

Our third technique is no technique at all—lacking time, to let them fall. We have, in the past, when good, clean straw was available, packed a thick mulch under the plants, after cultivating once or twice. This also serves to prevent splashback—which in gardener's lingo simply describes the habit of hard rain bouncing back after hitting the hard surface of summer soil. The leaves of tomato plants are sensitive and highly susceptible to fungus and disease. Tomatoes prefer to receive water at the plant base, not on the leaves. We are told by literature and horticulturists to avoid handling tomato plants when they are wet, as Sarah S., one-time Quail Hill worker and tomato lover, reminded me, repeatedly. On a wet, wet summer I was barred from the tomato patch.

Oddly, during this summer of constant rain, we have harvested a fine crop of fruit, forty-four varieties in all. In the growing field where we let them ramble, we kept them well weeded, and we plucked the fruit every other day, tossing the culled fruit for the benefit of nearby crows. A few days of sun, when the plants are at their peak, may alter a failed season into a season of sweetness.

Reportedly, Ben Q.'s favorite was Brandywine, a pink tomato of good size, unusual shape, and superb taste. We have grown this indeterminate variety, which can take ninety days to ripen, for ten years at Quail Hill, and the performance varies, according to the weather. Given the number of choices, one of the thrills of tomato growing is selection; the names are fascinating, as are the tales. Radiator Charlie's Mortgage Lifter, another plant with sizable fruit, has found a secure home in our tomato patch. M. C. Byles, or Radiator Charlie, who owned a repair shop at the foot of a steep hill, and had no formal education, created this tomato by crossbreeding the four largest fruits he could find. He planted one variety in the center of a circle, and with a baby's ear syringe he crossed that plant with pollen from the others; the following year he planted the finest seedling in the center, and selected again. After six years he had a stable variety, large-fruited and full of taste, and he began selling his delicious tomatoes, one dollar per plant (during the 1940s). In six years' time Radiator Charlie had paid off the mortgage on his home!

Before recommending further enticing tomato varieties, let me discuss some cultural details. Tomatoes, of course, love good soil rich in organic matter, but they will also do well in a sandy medium enriched with compost. (If you cast tomato scraps into the compost heap, you will be treated to a selection of volunteer sprouts come spring.) Like other nightshades, tomatoes do not require a high pH (6.0 will do), but they do need available phosphorus. An excess of fresh manure or nitrogen will produce a lot of greenery, but a shortage of fruit. For our local soils, Bridgehampton silt loam, the critical requirement is calcium. For years we made use of a liquid calcium chelate, to treat the soil and as a foliar feed, but we found that we needed something more. Now, with the help of volunteers, we add a cup of bonemeal, at the base of each plant, as we are transplanting into the soil. Multiply this action by some thousands and you will sense a definite determination to succeed in the game of tomato production.

Lacking adequate calcium, tomatoes are sure to develop blossom end rot—ruined!—just when you thought you would enjoy a juicy tomato. The other cause of this persistent problem is an uneven supply of water, so we pray to the heavens for consistency. Fish emulsion, applied at the base of the plant, or used to dip the plants in before setting out, is fortifying, as is well-aged compost, incorporated into the soil prior to planting out. I am always amazed to watch the first nightshades put out in late May. They maintain a stasis, as if saddened to be cast out of the comfort of the greenhouse or cold frame, until, after several weeks, some ancient cellular memory clicks that possibly summer "is icumen in."

It certainly frightens me that the catalogue on my desk lists eighteen abbreviations for disease identification purposes. All experienced tomato growers, I'm sure, have been forced to open to the glossy display pages of "Identifying Diseases of Plants." Early blight and alternaria are frequent problems, as is fusarium wilt, which is caused by a soil fungus. Late blight, which can occur under humid or moist conditions, will devastate all members of the nightshade family, overnight. Long Island potato farmers, knowing that late blight spores can travel one quarter mile on the wind, tremble at the mention of it. To avoid these problems, and others, the farmer or gardener must know his or her soil, research and choose disease-resistant varieties, plant only the finest-looking specimens, and rotate to another place in the garden each year. Under our rotation system, essential planning for organic growing, no member of the nightshade family will return to the same spot for at least four years. I have known several farmers who rotate all crops, except tomatoes—and I have heard the argument that tomatoes love to feed upon themselves, year after year. Words to this effect make me extremely nervous; I prefer to find new ground for this trickster plant.

We have learned to take our time with tomatoes, in the spring. The anxious horticulturist, eager to get the seeding under way, will find herself, come May, with plants crisscrossing to the ceiling of the greenhouse or window bay. We prefer to seed later, say in the beginning of April, so that when the day arrives for setting out in the field, our nightshades are small, but strong and healthy. Each year we trial some new varieties, following advice from those who fancy the love apple. Our annual Tomato Tasting, traditionally held at the start of September, with a rating scale ranging from "The Best" to "Yuk," also serves as an ordering sheet for the following year. In addition to the very popular cherries, several varieties consistently score top grades, and the tasters are amazed by the variations in size, color, and texture. Green Zebra is sweet, pretty, and prolific; Garden Peach is a beautiful yellow with rose color, and yes, the skin is fuzzy. The black tomatoes (mahogany, really) vary each year, though we always plant Cherokee Purple, Paul Robeson (the Russians loved the singer, and they love black tomatoes), and Black Plum—wonderful for drying or sauce. There is a place in every garden for grand, ugly fruits, so we continue to plant Striped German, Persimmon, and Omar's Lebanese. Moskvich ripens early, and rarely cracks, and each year we harvest an abundance of Arkansas Traveler, Rutgers, and the orange Valencia. Throughout this season we feasted in the field on Jaune Flammée and Juliet. And we harvested thousands of pounds of Amish Paste, Red Agate, Aunt Mary's, and Gilbertie, to be made into sauce in the kitchens of the Ross School, to accompany a school year of pasta.

My older son has recently acquired a taste for fresh tomatoes, after eighteen years of hesitation. My younger children, connoisseurs of sauce, still refuse to taste the fruit picked from the vine. I, myself, a slow, reluctant student of tomato culture, now reassure the members of our farm that, yes, we will seed more of them, and harvest more of them, and we will search for the sweetest of the heirlooms. When the rains are sparse, I turn to the clouds to persuade them to part, at least once a week. If the clouds open up day after day, I remind the heavens that tomatoes found their natural home in Italy— they prefer the sun. I recall these words, with respect for the wolf's peach, the love apple, the apple of paradise: "Anyone would be a fool to take the sun lightly. . . ."

ERUTAN

Swallows adore the bamboo tips of our bean teepees, stopping their flight to perch above the three sisters—corn, beans, and squash. Such elegant birds in their flight and feeding, they sail in and out just over rye grass or young corn, often weaving a continuous thread that surrounds the tractor when we turn soil or mow a meadow. They are moving through now, on a flight to somewhere, but for an afternoon we cultivate together, or taste the same salt air, intimate with the community of grasses and loam, beetles, bees, oaks, carrots, yarrow, clouds.

The kids are on their way to the farm from Mary Ryan's. When they arrive Lisa will properly introduce us—standing in a circle, facing each other—and then we'll forage through the fields, talking and tasting. For children who have never been outside a city the experience can be a kind of revelation. We visit the beehives—thousands of workers winging in and out—and then whisk over to the chicken shed. Here, Raymond, once inside the pandemonium of sound and flutter, is calmed beyond measure by the physical contact with a feathered creature. I like this about hens—it does not take long for children especially to locate the common ground.

Ten years ago Ann Crutcher called me from California: "We're looking for a place on the East Coast to set up a camp for inner city kids who live in foster homes . . . would the Peconic Land Trust have a site we could use?"

At the time the land allocated to the community farm did not seem ideal for camping. I called Mary Ryan, owner of Fireplace Farm, eighteen acres situated on the bluffs in Springs, a piece of the South Fork that hugs Long Island Sound, her dwelling the last stop on Springs Fireplace Road. The name derives from the bluffs that Mary now owns, and that the PLT has protected through a conservation easement. Early settlers of East Hampton, in order to communicate with the residents of Gardiner's Island one half mile across the water of the bay, lit fires on the high land above the beach: Fireplace Farm. Years ago, Mary, having heard of the community farm and of our organic experiment, approached us: "Are you able and willing to farm another field? I don't enjoy being fallow."

Mary agreed to meet with Lisa Tanzman, who has directed Camp Erutan (read it backwards) for eighteen years. The result of this fruitful conversation: for the past nine years Lisa has set up camp at Fireplace Farm (once a girls' summer camp) to benefit children placed in foster care, often uniting siblings separated in the foster care process. They come for two weeks to sleep in tents under the stars, to harvest at Quail Hill, to cook out in the open, to spend some time in the waters of the Sound and the Atlantic, and to pass the nights with a clear view of Cassiopeia and the Big Dipper.

In 1987 Lisa took six kids for three days into the Los Osos valley of California to camp out in teepees. The toughest six-year-old from the city had the toughest time in his encounter with nature. Another child told Lisa, "Be patient with him." She gave him, in her words, "Patience, kindness, and someone to trust." The transformation was so complete that Lisa thought, "If this child can be so affected by the natural world, if he can so radically change, so can anyone." Three days led to two weeks, to four weeks, to six weeks, to a camp, here, on the East Coast, on the bluffs of Fireplace Farm.

Now Lisa imagines a new alternative for foster children—the Erutan Community—with a goal of keeping siblings together. Children who have been removed from their homes and cannot be reunited with their biological families nor adopted will be given a permanent home, both a safe haven and a place to return to. Lisa writes:

> It is important for children to know they have a voice—and to know how to use it. The Erutan Community will help children break the potential cycle of abuse and social dependency, which has for too many families become an intergenerational tradition at great cost to the larger community as to themselves personally.

The model for this community, in the works right now, will also incorporate the Erutan parent center, with the hope of rehabilitating parents to create the chance for families to be reunited.

On their visit to Quail Hill the children are introduced to carrots in the ground, an abundance of spuds in hills under our silt loam, and Matt's Wild Cherry tomatoes, sweeter than Snickers, right off the vine. I am left with a packet of drawings of lettuces, cabbage, workers in the field, the queen of the bees, the tire swing under a great beech tree, and "hen-baby" in the coop. The children leave, I believe, with a deeper, more secure sense of the unpredictable, fertile, wild world of Erutan. John Hay reminds us that the word "nature" has a Latin root that translates as "to be born."

Now the smiling farmer has to leap into another kind of action. It's summer—substitute the word "slide" for "transition," the time when thing after thing cries out for attention. I climb onto the Case 265 for another afternoon in the sun, cultivating plants. The "offset" tractor is fitted with a tool bar on the belly of the machine—the driver can easily look down rather than over his shoulder to judge the distance between plant and steel shank. It is not easy to teach or discuss the details of cultivation—one must simply mount the tractor, cast an eye toward the crop, read the soil conditions, and pray

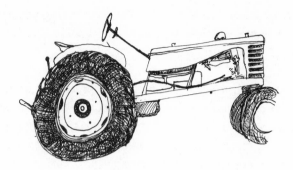

for some luck. It is likely that the training period will involve broc-coli plants flopping over in the sun, onion bulbs uprooted, squash plants sagging in the rows, and the tops of potato plants all falling over to the south. After a year or two—and countless hours on the Case—the driver is almost professional, and perhaps capable of uniting in one thought the root structure of plants, the friability of silt loam, and the action of hydraulics.

Having traversed row after row of potatoes, tomatoes, and au-tumn squash, the steel shanks (or shoes) under the belly of the Case sparkle. And after cultivation the plants show appreciation—they seem to leap forward or upward, liberated from close contact with competing vegetation (weeds). At a certain point in the growing season many plants tend to shade out the soil at their base, thus pre-venting the germination of unwanted seeds. But we're not there yet—so for now cultivation is a weekly or twice-weekly occupation, everywhere where seeds or seedlings take up space.

This is also the time of year when machinery and implements—used on a rigorous daily basis—have an increased tendency to sput-ter or stall or separate, or, alas, give up the ghost. Of course there are numerous proactive measures to prepare for this seasonal frenzy, but every farmer knows what it means to be thrown into the reactive mode. The favored response is to react and repair and re-turn to the field; at times the only choice is to pedal backwards while searching for the forward gear.

Listen to what E. B. White has to say concerning the avocation. In the course of his review of a book entitled *Practical Farming for Beginners* he comments,

> Mr. Highstone, being himself a practicing farmer, knows one important truth about country life: he knows that farming is about twenty percent agriculture and eighty percent mending something that has got busted. Farming is a sort of glorified repair job. This is a truth that takes some people years to discover, and many farmers go their whole lives without ever really grasping the idea. A good farmer is nothing more nor less than a handy man with a sense of humus.

This week, in rapid succession, the generator used to power the pump for irrigation split apart, we were greeted with flat tires on two tractors and one mower, the trusty 1989 Jeep refused to depart from the farm shop lot, and the Buddingh finger weeder dropped an essential part of the cultivating apparatus. Tires are costly, but in exchange for a gift of radishes Jerry of Consumer Tire is ever willing to serve us with some speed. It is difficult to say good-bye to the sporty Jeep, but we're lucky to have a lumbering GMC as the old/new packhorse. The generator has proven to be a test even for Sid Colum, our local genius welder, capable of joining together anything made of metal. We had to convince him that the finger weeder—which resembles a medieval torture device—actually has a relevant purpose. The arm of the implement, which snapped at a point of stress, is fitted with circular tubing decorated with strong spokes that radiate out from the center. When the implement is lowered to touch the soil, the spokes revolve to uproot and smother unsuspecting weeds. The sooner we repair it the cleaner our fields will be and the more intact will be my sense of humus.

At this time of year, without the benefit of sheep to crop them, the grasses indigenous to this place grow with a summer vigor. One member of the crew is kept occupied mowing the aisles, under the fences, around the windrows of compost. When my oldest son, Levin, was here it was his job to mow the orchard. Now as you enter the valley by the farm track there is a mowed path that weaves through wild brambles and bittersweet, the entrance to the path just barely visible. When I am not driven to plow this, seed that, cultivate this, I allow myself to amble onto this grass walkway. I am reminded of a certain meandering stream outside of Oxford, the Windrush, where I often walked.

Levin made this path one summer, straying on the mower from his appointed task—to mow the orchard. He mowed his way through the thick wild grass and vines until he reached the rutted farm track, where the mower stopped, wheels suspended over a rut. Embarrassed, he had to find his father, who had to tow him out, grumbling, "Why would you drive into the brambles . . . huh?" But now is my chance to acknowledge the gift—a series of casual walks throughout the summer, noting the changing wild growth, butterfly weed, honeysuckle, bittersweet berries, monarchs on milkweed, lost for a few meandering moments on a narrow path through the wild. My thought is—I should encourage him to stray again, to break at various times from the orchard pattern, row after row. If you visit this place I will point you toward Levin's path—look up to catch the liquid flight of swallows, step by step on this soil listen for the music of wind as it weaves a thread through the brambles.

BEEPING AT CROWS

They appear out of nowhere, though immediately the air absorbs the musical motion of their flight. Above the noise of the diesel tractor, the feeding flight of swallows, like notes rising and falling, creates a meadow music. I am there to mow a field; they arrive to catch the flush of insects that rise out of the grasses. Their undulating flight suggests that we are at sea, though I feel the solid wheels of the tractor beneath me. This rich soil supports my weight, the weight of timothy and clover and ragweed, and also the weightlessness of swallows. Row after row I follow the dance of birds who benefit from my labor; part of the broad circle that involves the soil, we act in time, together.

We are mowing often now, when crops are "over the hill" or harvested, in preparation for the autumn cover cropping. Expecting rain, two days ago we prepared several fields to be seeded with a late-summer mixture of bellbeans, oats, and buckwheat. Soon we will note a carpet of green, as the oats and buckwheat jump up, and later the deeper green of the legumes known as bellbeans (a field version of fava beans), sown to provide a supply of nitrogen for the crops to follow. Buckwheat grows to a height of a few feet within the oat mixture, blossoms white, and then, along with the oats, dies back during the winter. In spring we plow the residue, a superb source of organic matter, back into our Amagansett loam. Corn stalks, bean beetles, fat radish roots, red-root pigweed, purslane—all turned back into the layer of humus, food for earthworms and microbes, organic matter for sprouting buckwheat and oats, foundation for our food.

I've just returned from the autumn squash patch—these cucurbits, beginning to ripen now, loved the last rain. We are now harvesting the first fruits from this patch, the variety known as Pasta, a spaghetti squash. Soon, with the cool of the night, buttercups, sugarloaf, delicata, and red kuri will sweeten, as pumpkins turn a fine color in the far field. The first leeks, kale, Chinese cabbage, potatoes (red, white, and blue), Silver Queen corn, and peppers of color all ripen within the "mellow fruitfulness" of the season.

This has been the year of the cucumber and the crow. Planted by hand at the right moment in the right soil, when soil temperature had risen to 65 degrees or so, cultivated carefully, and washed with abundant rains, Marketmore, Suyo Long, Little Leaf, Lemon, and Boothbay Blonde have flourished, sheltered by the sunflowers. At the beginning of this year, Ellen C., farm member and lover of cukes, remembering another abundant year, pointed to the far corner of the Deep Lane field: "Cucumbers love to grow out there, you know. . . ."

In another field, to the south of Town Lane, where we have bedded down tomatoes, peppers, eggplant, broccoli, sprouts, and late cauliflower—it is here the crows dominate. Whenever I have the chance to be in this field with the cultivating tractor I take up the chase, racing from one planting patch to another, beeping wildly (the Case 265 horn is particularly high-pitched). The crows, bold and blocky, shaped like the pepper varietal Fat and Sassy, seem amused, but basically unconcerned. They repeatedly find temporary lodging atop the cedars or among the sassafras trees. To date these crows, joined by cousin pheasants and a growing herd of deer, have eaten 95 percent of our sweet corn, and a fair share of tomatoes and various other nightshades. The field is bordered with an electrified deer fence, and the birds casually descend through the "bird scare" tape and a battery of pots and pans and utensils carefully arranged by apprentices Jessica and Chuck. I warned that this musical clothesline was no match for a well-trained crowd of crows, acrobatic and irascible, but I also intend to encourage apprentice ingenuity. Investigating, I learned that *Corvus brachyrhynchos* has a high reproductive capacity and is virtually omnivorous. When I complained to my young son Liam that I had asked the crows to simply share some of the food with us (given that we planted it), he replied, logically, "They can't talk to people, or understand them . . . if they could, they would probably share!"

I have not always viewed the crow as a foe, and in fact my painter mother-in-law, whom I respect, has always had a deep affection for these black birds. When I lived on the Cornish hillside, each day was another occasion to marvel at a cousin of the crow, the slightly smaller and more polite jackdaw. The Studio in which we lived (Love Lane Studio) was originally built to house a wood sculptor, Pog Yglesias, and her avian friends. There was a simple wooden box that rested atop the exposed wooden rafters, within the living space, home to Nevermore, a jackdaw who lived with Pog for fifteen years, an intelligent friend who slipped in and out of the bay window, which was always open. Nevermore, who had fallen down a chimney in the village of Mousehole, had been rescued by lads and brought to be healed by the "bird ladies" who lived on Love Lane.

When we first arrived on the hillside, in 1981, we were visited daily by former Mousehole bird sanctuary patients, probably in search of the caring ladies. Jackdaws are incredible fliers, at home in the difficult and dangerous wind currents that batter and rise off the steep granite cliffs of the Penwith peninsula, but also at home on the windowsill. They are all black, but their heads shimmer with silvery feathers, so that they somewhat resemble the court jester. Because they were familiar with the Studio, which was next door to the sanctuary, a number of jackdaw guests would tap daily at the window, and proceed to eat out of our hands. Dorothy, until she died at age ninety, fed them twice a day, next door at Love Lane Cottage, in a bird porch of her design. Her guests were especially fond of buttered bread—the granary loaf to be exact.

When the breeze picked up, a flock of jackdaws would appear out of nowhere to flip and soar just offshore, above the cliffs. They were at play—comical feathered fliers whipping through the air as if hurled by a tornado. Though I grew vegetables for years in the cliff meadows above the village, I do not remember a single raid on my garden by a jackdaw.

Because the cliff meadows extended right up to the edge and over the lip of granite rock, poised one hundred feet above the surf, I often stopped there after turning ground or planting, to gaze out at the Lizard Point or to compose. I have always thought that the melodic lines spoken by Edgar in *King Lear* were imagined by Shakespeare after a visit to this particular headland. Gloucester, blinded and hopeless, is led to the very brim of a steep cliff at his request, by his son Edgar, disguised as Poor Tom. Edgar speaks:

> The crows and choughs that wing the midway air
> Show scarce so gross as beetles. Halfway down
> Hangs one that gathers samphire—dreadful trade;
> Methinks he seems no bigger than his head.
> The fishermen that walk upon the beach
> Appear like mice; and yond tall anchoring bark,
> Diminished to her cock; her cock, a buoy
> Almost too small for sight. The murmuring surge
> That on the unnumbered idle pebbles chafes
> Cannot be heard so high.

The chough is a jackdaw. The irony of the scene, not lost on a gardener, is that father and son are standing on flat ground. The eloquence of Edgar's speech convinces the tired old man, who leaps; Edgar "discovers" him on the beach, and exclaims, "Thy life's a miracle."

Between planting and cultivating potatoes in the hillside meadows, and watching the jackdaws' sport, standing on firm soil, I often
recalled Shakespeare's lines, with Edgar's veiled message. Years
later, working the soil on another peninsula, I try to savor some respect for another *Corvus*—one that wings the midway air in the direction of my melons and tomatoes. Here, beeping at crows and
berating them appear to be hopeless, and I accept my son Liam's
logic. As an alternative persuasion, and recognizing that we are part
of the same community, I wrote a poem, which considers crows in
another season. I recited it to them, as a kind of peace offering:

PEPPER AND SALT

Unaware of their place among ice
and the white blanket of being
over the field, late sun singing

in branches heavy with March,
beech buds waving
as wrapped feathers in air,

to the idea of space
these three surrender
and define color, marking

in a white circle
backed by cedars,
brush points, strokes of black,

marking snow, rye grass and sky
with their name: Crow!

And by the way, Crows! there is a field far away, over there! ripening with corn.

The mowing is done. I step down from the tractor to wade in

the cuttings, and to absorb the fresh, sweet smell of mown grass. In the streaming light I can see a full flush of insects and the quick rise and fall of swallows. Now that our improvisation is interrupted, one by one the swallows dive for a final feed and then fly into the far reaches of the broad circle. And as farming is filled with purpose, I turn to the next task, wearing the aroma of timothy and clover.

ARC OF THE INVISIBLE

Today a west wind fans the backs of apple leaves in the orchard, and the air is wet over planted fields. A diffuse sea light defines our place—we are surrounded by water. Green reappears in grass, stem, and cover crop. Vine crops love the return of sun; we have a fine patch of autumn and winter squash ripening at our field on Town Lane. Now, while the ground is warm and slightly moist, we are planting greens for early autumn, and some late beets and carrots, as seed heads mature on the rows of Autumn Beauty *Helianthus*.

When the last hard rain came, Graham H. and I slipped into slickers, grabbed several sacks of ancient seed (soybeans, oats, pasture mix), and proceeded to block the path of the runaway water that rushed toward the greenhouse in the valley. Inside, assisted by fans, Carpathian garlic and Stuttgarter onions were drying; we could not allow a flash flood to dampen the alliums. Our effort may have had little effect, but it was invigorating to slosh about in the instant river. After years of drought summers I welcome the risk associated with the liquid element.

During fifteen years of farming on the South Fork I have lived through five droughts, and I will admit to a preference for the opposite. We have in the past been forced to water-in crops in late May, and though it is rarely done, we have watered-in a cover crop in October, before the birds could devour all of the seed (we allow them a certain portion). I have been told that formerly South Fork farmers could survive without a deep well or a system of irrigation; for farmers on the North Fork of Long Island, irrigation has long been a necessity. The decade of the 1990s altered the pattern; it is now imperative for any grower on Long Island to be prepared to assist the heavens. The methodology may vary but the need exists, and the farmer can hear an insistent refrain, even in sleep: "Plants love water, plants love water. . . ."

For those who work daily outside, and whose livelihood is influenced by patterns of weather, the moment of transition after, say, a month of anticipation can be dramatic almost beyond description. During one of the drought years, after forty days without rain, I still recall the first, singular, heavy drops, followed by a full day of rain, and then, at the close of day, a rainbow.*

> "I am off for the end of the rainbow," replied Brer Anansi, looking up at the big, beautiful rainbow.
> "To the end of the rainbow?" repeated Brer Buzzard.
> "But that is a very long journey. I have often tried flying there but there seems to be no end to that colorful band in the skies. What are you going there for, by the way?"

I am bending to harvest squash, peppers, and celery in the far field, when over the stalks of corn seven colors appear, arcing against a steel sky that burns silver in the late light. This is the first Long Island rainbow I have seen to equal those of the Cornish sky—a show of color, then an intensity of color upon color. Light translates water in air to a blue and violet ink, marking the moving clouds. Under this arc the field is illuminated. Ordinary beet greens, brassicas, parsnips, and rutabagas reflect the deepening colors of the air. This transition is a multiple event—from drought to rainfall, and from deep summer into autumn.

---

*Listen to the conversation—between spider and bird—concerning the most beautiful rainbow in the world, from David Makhanlall's *The Best of Brer Anansi*.

We listen with an equal intensity, at times of seasonal transition, to whatever informs the life of a particular place. Here, sometimes the wind dominates, or perhaps the ocean mist, or the mimic catbird, at times the persistent flush of nutsedge attempting to seed, or a sudden event that claims the sky. A crowd of dragonflies fills the air around the sunflowers, bees are busy on the hedge of raspberries. The sassafras trees burn with the orange light leaping out of the west.

Now we enter into autumn. The late light still finds green in leaves and the beech undergrowth. I watch as the red clover, which we sowed under the corn in July, twines up through the mown corn. Pumpkins, butternuts, and sweet dumplings lie in rows, curing in the cool air. To plant and to reap is part of what defines the human community. The nearer one is to this—breaking apart a bulb to plant, kneeling in loam to transplant broccoli, sifting together seeds of buckwheat, clover, and Japanese millet for a cover—the nearer one is to the changes of air and water and light that work like spells to define a place. Seven colors suddenly appear in the sky—part of a day or season, and arc of the invisible, that at times translates into indigo. The journey's end is here in the field, and I name it: rainbow, rainbow, rainbow.

AUTUMN

Autumn has turned the dark trees toward the hill;
The wind has ceased; the air is white and chill.
Red leaves no longer dance against your foot,
The branch reverts to tree, the tree to root.

And now in this bare place your step will find
A twig that snaps flintlike against the mind;
Then thundering above your giddy head,
Small quail dart up, through shafting sunlight fled.

Like brightness buried by one's sullen mood
The quail rise startled from the threadbare wood;
A voice, a step, a swift sun-thrust of feather
And earth and air come properly together.

—WILLIAM JAY SMITH,
"QUAIL IN AUTUMN," 1937

THE WANDERER

This year the milkweed climbed to a fantastic height in our valley, a result of continuous rainfall. This is the first year since we acquired our Ag-Rain Water Wheel that this staple instrument of summer has actually remained in the barn. In search of bags of lime or gypsum, or other tools, we were forced to climb over the invaluable water wheel, all summer. Please, I am not complaining. Although we receive a sufficient supply of yearly rain—forty-two inches is our annual average—we often encounter long dry periods during the height of the growing season. Throughout our first decade this farm experienced four summers of drought, which led to endless consternation, and the eventual purchase of over a thousand feet of pipe and hardware and the transportable water wheel. Given the effort that irrigation demands, I prefer wet weather. And from my experience, within reason of course, plants love water.

Late this spring, one member, astonished at the robust flowers of milkweed, refused to accept my identification of the plant. The flower looks somehow out of place; it resembles a Christmas ornament on a summer plant, an orb studded and sparkling with white cloves. It is difficult to see the connection between the flower and the trait that more prominently proclaims, "Milkweed!" This is the teardrop-shaped seedpod, stuffed with cottonlike seed wings that develop in early autumn. These seedpods are a favorite of children, and the young of heart, when we take a discovery walk around the farm. Break open the rough seedpod, and the magic of procreation is revealed—a myriad of seeds, each with a wing of fluff, delicate and light, ready for a ride on the wind.

Many farmers would protect their cropping fields from the spread of such "weed" seeds, by mowing or eradicating. Instead, through the time-honored practice of passive resistance, we allow some wild plants to flourish and reproduce in certain areas, sometimes adjacent to our cultivated plantings. I like to think that we are providing a homestead for wild cultivars, though I am aware of the inherent delusion—who am I to claim even a modicum of control? No matter who claims command, uncultivated, wild, so-called natural areas invite beneficial insects to befriend our organic experiments. Such a style of gardening or farm management can provide essential nourishment to particular insects. If allowed to stand and reproduce, milkweed will provide food for that perennial favorite, the monarch butterfly. Monarchs, of the family Danaiinae, feed on the milky substance that courses through the stem of *Asclepius*. The monarch has developed an immunity to this poisonous latex, which is toxic enough to produce a heart attack in a small animal. The monarch caterpillar does not digest the latex, but instead stores it; the poison stays intact in the body of the butterfly, throughout its migratory journey.

Multiple generations, overlapping, perhaps six in all, cooperate to make the annual journey a reality. As they travel, female adults lay eggs on the milkweed plants that will be the sole food for their offspring, the brightly colored caterpillars. When the eggs hatch, the next generation continues the cycle of feeding and flight and finding home. The sap of milkweed is their advantage when they sprout wings and take to the airstream. The mythology we have inherited from Ovid's *Metamorphoses* is embodied in the annual maturation cycle of this butterfly. It has recently been called the most beloved insect on earth, evidenced by the numerous orchestrated efforts to protect habitat and homing grounds. Robert Michael

Pyle, who compiled his findings into *Chasing Monarchs: Migrating with the Butterflies*, followed the monarch's path for over nine thousand miles. For those who feel for and follow the plight of this insect, the field of study embraces the North American continent. This year our local farm feeding stations were full of fuel for the annual migration.

Several years ago, because of a favorable weather pattern, we watched, for days, thousands of monarchs fly low over our fields, apparently hugging the coastline, stopping to feed on buckwheat and the offerings of the wild. The air just above our field crops was a fluttering tide of orange and black, a delicate flow of wings on the currents of late summer. Buckwheat in full blossom, on its own, is a beautiful sight; speckled with the wings of monarchs, an agonomic crop transforms into an impressionistic painting. It is almost impossible to imagine that these tiny creatures can and will propel themselves another three thousand miles to the south, so that the species will survive. When they float, or flutter, by, or land on thin stems we can only think—frailty. But this colorful, determined, acrobatic insect is capable of traveling one hundred miles a day to return to certain branches in the Sierra Pelon and Sierra Chincua mountains of Mexico.

It was not until the 1970s that this winter home was discovered, but by 1976 the migratory monarch was elevated to the status of "endangered phenomenon." Although one of the most widespread butterflies in the world, the monarch is the subject of a conservation campaign, an attempt to ensure the safety of its vast habitat. At home in the oyamel forests of Mexico, still, year after year, in pupae, in rest, the next generation begins its journey north.

After days of rain, I climb Quail Hill, our 110-foot-tall Long Island mountain, to be in the center of two lights—the autumn moon rising in the east, the sun setting opposite. I stop to examine an open milkweed pod—seed and seed wings wet and holding to the cupped shape, perhaps waiting for the right moment to dislodge and take hold somewhere else. If we continue to preserve pockets of wildness even within a cultivated landscape, we also help to preserve a sustenance for the monarch butterfly, whose flyway extends for thousands of miles. I bend to detach a seedpod, and with a flick of the wrist I offer seed wings a chance for a patch of hillside. If the seed takes and a plant matures, the creature to benefit, also known as the wanderer, will bear golden wings.

"SING HUZZAH FOR THE LIFE OF THE SOILED WORM!"

I've been a participant on the interview circuit lately, after several visits to my son's school this autumn. My habit is to enter classrooms carrying a box of farm and garden supplies—packets of seeds, pots of soil mix, leaves and straw, compost, worm castings. Judging by the requests for interviews, I seem to have sparked some interest in matters of the soil.

Sam K., aged ten, with an assignment to select a particular ecosystem to study, chose to report on a farmland ecosystem; he photographed the farm as I introduced him to the wild and the cultivated. Noel, aged eight, was required to prepare questions concerning occupational choices and routine. But his real interest is earthworms. He listed his questions on a single page, with space for the farmer's answers. I was immediately reminded of an introductory page to *Geography III*, by Elizabeth Bishop:

From *First Lessons in Geography*,
Monteith's Geographical Series,
A. S. Barnes & Co., 1884

LESSON VI
What is Geography?
    A description of the earth's surface.
What is the Earth?
    The planet or body on which we live.

What is the shape of the Earth?
Round, like a ball.
Of what is the Earth's surface composed?
Land and water.

One of the most discerning poets of the twentieth century reminds her readers of beauty in simplicity, in this case to be found in
the spare, accurate language of a primer.

Noel had printed, with careful lettering: "Where do earthworms
live? What do they eat? How long do they live?" It is my guess that
few people could provide the answers to his questions, despite the
fact that the contribution by earthworms to the health of our soils is
incalculable.

Charles Darwin was long fascinated by earthworms, and he
chose to keep an assortment of flowerpots, each with a resident
worm, atop his piano. He learned that when he played the low
notes of the instrument, any worm feeding on the soil surface
would disappear down into its burrow. Darwin concluded that the
earthworms "felt" the vibration of the bass notes as they would feel
under the soil the approach of an enemy. Soft and juicy as a bodily
quality may aid in locomotion, but it also attracts predators.

It is estimated that almost 200,000 earthworms can reside in an
acre of soil. That's 199,999 more than occupied our hillside field
when we took it over. That one factor—the seeming total absence
of this creature from our prime agricultural soil—led me to pursue
research concerning soil depletion and soil fertility. Earthworms improve fertility because they aid in the formation of humus, but they
also turn over the earth. As a matter of agricultural practice, we have
not really solved the complex problem at the heart of farming—
tillage. How do we plow the earth and still retain the best of it, topsoil, while protecting against erosion and loss of organic matter?
According to Peter Warshall, in an article entitled "Tilth and Tech-
nology," included in *The Fatal Harvest Reader*, "Since 1950, about one
third of American cropped land has had to be abandoned because of

erosion problems." Improper use of the moldboard plow, introduced in 1837 by John Deere, and a reliance on inorganic salt fertilizers have accelerated the depletion of our soils. This is despite the
warnings of soil conservationists and organic researchers from the
early days of the twentieth century. As soil structures break down
and land is susceptible to erosion, a self-destructive cycle ensues.
The life within a soil, from microbes to earthworms, essential to
the cycle of revitalization, instead continues to diminish. The high-
input industrial approach, after some early success with improved
yields, has led to a virtual desertification of some of our richest
soils. The newest wave in conventional agriculture—the introduction of bioengineered crops, from zero United States acres planted
in 1995 to more than one hundred million United States acres in
2003—is flowing forth, like a river swollen to the banks with industrial ambition, with no understanding of how this will affect soil
ecology. Peter Warshall observes, "Given the complexity of soils
and the ability of microbes to disperse explosively, the need to go
slow cannot be overemphasized."

When I descend from the Case tractor to inspect the soil on the
hill, after I have dragged the chisel plow through, I am encouraged.
The soil has some crumble to it (microscopic creatures need air!),
and here and there earthworms have agreed to inhabit the hillside.
How do they get here? We provide the living space, they arrive.

There is only one book in the Quail Hill Farm extended library that is not on loan, despite repeated requests by determined
students—*One-Straw Revolution*. There are a few books on the subject of farming—*Farmers of Forty Centuries* would be another—which
are considered classic, and this is one, long out of print. Masanobu
Fukuoka farmed on the island of Shikoku in southern Japan, using a
method others have called "natural farming" (with characteristic
humor he referred to his style as "do nothing farming"). He was
able to produce good yields of rice and mandarin oranges without
ever using a plow and without applying compost. He developed his
methods, after studying the ways of his local ecosystem, by what he

called cooperation with nature. In the years after Fukuoka gave up plowing, his fields actually improved in fertility, structure, and water-retention capabilities. He wrote, "Nature does not change, although the way of viewing nature invariably changes from age to age. No matter the age, natural farming exists forever as the wellspring of agriculture."

I mention Fukuoka here not because I believe his methods can be easily adopted, but because his style offers an alternative to tillage, the annual disruption of the soil complex. Farmers and gardeners everywhere can learn from his insight and respect for one strand of straw.

Out on the prairie of this North American continent, another holistic experiment is under way, under the leadership of Wes Jackson. For over twenty years the Land Institute, based in Salina, Kansas, has been researching what it refers to as "Natural Systems Agriculture." The design for this revolution in agriculture is based upon a switch in focus—from annual planting cycles to a mixture of perennials. From what I can tell from a distance, the intention is in sympathy with the "natural farming" techniques developed by Fukuoka. The stated mission of the Land Institute begins, "When people, land, and community are as one, all three members prosper; when they relate not as members but as competing interests, all three are exploited." Jackson wrote a paper in 1978 in which he advocated for "an agriculture based on the way the prairie works." The key to this "alternative" approach to farming—which is really based on centuries of undocumented research—is to acknowledge nature as "the equal mother." Central to the work of the Land Institute is an intensive breeding program, intended to discover plant material that is vigorous and adaptable, and to understand how natural cycles can return fertility to land. Wes Jackson, in a foreword to *Farming in Nature's Image*, quotes from Liberty Hyde Bailey's *The Holy Earth*: "A good part of agriculture is to learn how to adapt one's work to nature." At the Land Institute they look beyond short-term solutions toward a sustainable agriculture that is integrated with natural cycles; it is their particular focus to blend ecology and agriculture to create a perennial polyculture that mimics the prairie ecosystem. From my coastal farm in the humid Northeast, I have my eye on those in the prairie who research and labor in support of the living soil.

"The ultimate goal of farming is not the growing of crops, but the cultivation and perfection of human beings," says Masanobu Fukuoka. As a community farm we cultivate relationships with students of all ages who have questions concerning our local soils and the flora and fauna of the broader ecosystem. Sometimes the answers are surprising:

> *How long do earthworms live?*
> An earthworm can live for ten years.

It is the season when the students from my Friends' World College Agroecology class select a topic for the term research paper. During the course, which takes place on the farm, they are exposed to the spectrum of cultural practices that define an organic farm, as well as a broad range of historical, political, and social issues involved with agriculture. One student is engaged by the controversy over GMOs, another will report on the medicinal properties of herbs, another is intrigued by biodynamics, one student will comb the historical literature. At some point in our seminar held in the field or orchard I will read a bit of verse to them, perhaps from Frost, or Wendell Berry, or Wordsworth, or Virgil, so that language with cadence is part of the weave of ecological dialogue.

The agroecology class was introduced to Quail Hill Farm by Hugh McGuinness, one of the most respected birders along Paumanock's shores; it was his idea to transport kids of college age out onto the farm, to explore sustainability, close up. When he left the college to take a teaching job elsewhere, I was asked to take over the course. I agreed, although I was unsure if we would be able to find the correct balance; could late-twentieth-century college students actually commit to academic study and farm labor, simultaneously? Could I keep an eye on the harvest, and prepare for class? Is it possible to introduce, in a brief semester, the plenitude a farmer comes to feel by working through the seasons in a single place? How would the farm, the community, and students enrolled in the class benefit?

Over the course of four or five years, six students have returned to work on the farm, several for the entire farming season, and I continue to receive calls and e-mails from around the globe; the connection with the land has been made. Heather M. returned to work and, eventually, to hold her wedding in the orchard. At the end of the term our root cellar is stacked with boxes of fat, mature carrots (thinned by students), rutabagas, celeriac (trimmed by students), cabbage, and spuds (gathered and packed by the class). To make the point, let me present a journal entry, and there are many more, from one former student, who knew how to do a day's work, and how to laugh:

> Monday, Dec. 13. The last day on the farm! I can't believe it. Inconceivable. We wanted to get Scott a present so we dug through our pockets and bags for gifts (most of them belonging to Scott in the first place) and Bob brought him an orange construction cone. We signed a black and white postcard of the early Rolling Stones, and Erin wrote a Haiku. Noting that the Rolling Stones postcard included the late, great, Brian Jones I wrote something to the effect of "Brian Jones rocks! But not as much as you." Love, BUNZA. Scott was overwhelmed by our fantastic gifts. We ate an early lunch consisting of squash, couscous, salad, and tofu. We then moved on to spinning honey, talking in a Southern accent, and singing the song which follows. This was the class that made me understand experiential education. I will never forget it. More immediately, however, I shant forget the jar of buckwheat honey in my dresser drawer. This is BUNZA signing off.

I was mildly surprised when Robert O., another student with a crisp sense of humor, approached me with a request to compose a research paper in verse, to be written jointly with Erin. "Well, I don't see why not," I said, "as long as the subject matter is derived from what we study in class." I was even more surprised to receive "The Sodyssey," an epic poem with the dubious subtitle "The Dirt on Soil," which begins:

> Sing hey for the life of an annelid!
> Sing ho for the life of a nightcrawler!
> Sing huzzah for the life of the soiled worm,
> Who himself sets the path he will follow!

Ten pages later, after meeting the guide Homer, Holy Moley, and Tillemachus, and after discussion of phosphorus ("potashes to potashes / dirt to dirt . . ."), boron, molybdenum, friability, fertility, humus, and loam, the epic closes with a rendition of "Farmer Scott's Compost Ballad": "Sing praises of compost, that organic stew/ The dirt from which everything grows." The term paper was accompanied by a taped rendition of the ballad, performed by the composers in an echoing room. Now I am honored to be a part of a brotherhood that includes Walt Whitman, but BUNZA was right— at the moment I was overwhelmed.

Agroecology is the study of the application of ecological concepts to the production of food. To conduct a college class on a farm—literally, in the field—of course disrupts the production cycle, but at the same time the culture of agriculture is reinvigorated. There is an exchange that favors the health of both land and people. Here is the song they sang while spinning honey in the farm shop:

SCOTT'S FARM
(set to the tune of "Maggie's Farm" by Bob Dylan):

I just wanna work on Scott's farm some more,
> Yeah, I just wanna work on Scott's farm some more,
I wake up in the morning and hope that it won't rain,

I got a head full of ideas that are driving me insane,
It's a shame the way I oversleep,
I just wanna work on Scott's farm some more,
I just wanna work on Quail Hill Farm some more,
Natalie and me didn't have much money,
While weeding we decided to take a vow,
It's got a bunch of chickens but it doesn't have a cow,
Yeah, I just wanna work on Quail Hill Farm some more,
Scott's a farmer and a professor and even writes poetry,
While weeding the raspberry patch I spent twenty minutes
    pulling out a tree,
It's a shame the way that nut grass grows,
I just wanna work on Scott's farm some more,
Yeah, I just wanna work with Tina and Matt some more,
Bob he was the driver with the help of Jae,
She should have brought the helmet each and every day,
It's a shame the way we ran out of gas,
I just wanna work on Scott's farm some more,
It's a shame the way the School of the Americas kept me
    away,
I just wanna work on Quail Hill Farm today,
Yeah, I just wanna work on Scott's farm some more,
Well I try my best to be the way I am,
But it takes five hours to cook with Dr. Clarjen,
He says: "Eat macrobiotically," I just get bored,
    'Cause I just wanna work on Scott's farm some more.

"SOILS ARE BEAUTIFUL!"

Whenever I am lucky enough to again see Sister Miriam McGillis, of Genesis Farm, I am reminded of words she spoke when I first met her: "To realize the health of a bioregion one must first measure the health of the top six inches of soil within that bioregion." I am also reminded of the soil scientist Hans Jenny, who could make his claim that "Soils are beautiful!" while looking at an apparently barren landscape. Jenny advises, "Ach! You must look with a fox's eyes!"

While Aldo Leopold wrote about the whole "circuit of soils, plants and animals," and "the interdependent community of living things," the poet William Blake did not hesitate to call this energy "eternal delight." A farmer might as well recall the liquid that pulses through root and stem of calendula, or the lively heat within a heap of compost, the flight of a fish hawk over the pond, or a steady succession of honeybees working the buckwheat.

I had the chance recently to listen again to a talk given by Marty Strange, founder of the Center for Rural Affairs, in Nebraska. Marty, in a keynote address, made claims for the extraordinary potential of CSA farms to develop new relationships, and he reminded those in the room of the brittle condition of mainstream, conventional agriculture. The audience for this timely replay of an address was made up of the students enrolled in my Friends' World College Agroecology course. The venue—upstairs in the shop at Quail Hill Farm, surrounded by books, seed packets, planning maps, and an array of earthy sculpture. A choice observation, delivered by Mr. Strange, left this class baffled.

Quoting the words of Leo Durocher, the colorful former manager of the New York Giants, Marty praised the glove worn by Willie Mays as "the place where triples go to die." My students were too young to be familiar with the center-field artistry of Willie Mays. I replayed the tape, and explained the grace of Willie on the field, because the analogy was critical.

In the course of discussing the value of land, Marty Strange noted that land is the place where the fruits of a farmer's labor "go to die." The statement is sobering, and the implications of a social policy that creates such a scenario are difficult to contemplate, and directly in opposition to the words of the influential horticulturist Liberty Hyde Bailey: "Equitable partition of land is the necessary basis of all self-sustaining agriculture." We only have to count the loss of farmland and farmers to acknowledge the reality. United States farmers now make up about one percent of the American population, and the average age of those still in the business is on the rise.

There are ways out of the dilemma, and the growth of Community Supported Agriculture throughout this country is among them. CSA, according to Marty and Robyn Van En, who started the first CSA in the country in Egremont, Massachusetts, in 1985, redefines the relationship between the producer and the consumer. Chuck Matthei, the brilliant and dear man who founded Equity Trust, proceeded further to say that the CSA model can also redefine the economics of the ownership of land. We now know, as Robyn knew, that family farms without strong, local markets cannot survive, nor can the land those families farm.

We know that risk sharing is a necessary and tricky business, and that it must be defined in relatively concrete terms—between producers and consumers—for CSAs to realize their true potential. This potential is based upon a partnership and a shared concern for the health of the soil, and the ensuing development of trust is antithetical to the mantra of consumerism: "No risk, no bother, no worry, no wait." The constant pressure of the market will always attempt to drive individual CSA farms toward a more conventional marketplace. And the market will tend to turn the CSA experiment into a movement both expensive and elite. In contrast, we now find innumerable examples of community farmers and their supporters who embrace a diversity of social justice issues, and who protect their capability to practice good land stewardship. Whether motivated by an ideal, by social conscience, or ethical belief, it is obvious that most CSAs reach out to help redefine community beyond the verges of the cornfield or the irrigation pond that waters melons, mizuna, and summer squash.

During the first meetings of northeastern community farmers, at the school in the Kimberton Hills of Pennsylvania, we would trade cultural secrets, and carefully discuss our salaries. The question of sustainability, we have come to find, also involves the rise and fall of global markets, affordable land, the tenure of marriages. I doubt that anyone guessed, as we watched the late winter light through the high windows of the school library, that ten or twelve years later there would be about 1,500 CSA farms throughout the country, that those farms would be active in cities, with projects for the homeless, or that an over-full farm wagon of apprentices would be ready to cultivate some new ground.

After listening again to the words of Marty Strange I recognize the necessity for advocates of sustainable agriculture to define "what we are for." Working together to forge partnerships, farmers, shareholders, policy makers, and extension agents can actually "afford" our concern for the health of the soil (most farmers, sadly, cannot afford to farm the best way they know how). Depending on how we choose to care for local soils, and that we save the best of it for cultivation, it can be possible for everyone, the haves and the have-nots, to gain access to land and good food. Chuck Matthei, gazing out at a crowd of dedicated conservationists, reminded us that, as yet, "not everyone is at the table." Stephen Decatur, of Live

Power Community Farm in California, has said, "Socially and eco-logically responsible agriculture also requires socially and economi-cally responsible land ownership. If equity and stewardship of land are shared by the community and the individual farmers . . . we can ensure that the land will remain in farming use and permanently af-fordable to farmers."

In a recent article entitled "Compromise, Hell!" Wendell Berry comments,

> Since the beginning of the conservation effort in our country, conservationists have too often believed that we could protect the land without protecting the people. This has begun to change, but for a while yet we will have to reckon with the old assumption that we can pre-serve the natural world by protecting wilderness areas while we neglect or destroy the economic landscapes— the farms and ranches and working forests—and the peo-ple who use them.

When the ocean breeze picks up, in the afternoon, I often watch the delicate dance of moths and beetles, wasps and honeybees, rest-ing and rising from millet and buckwheat and the sunflowers on the hill. One has to look with a fox's eyes to see in the grace of flight the determination of living beings—and they are equal to the wind, not greater or lesser, but equal, part of the community.

The sky has cleared, and so the agroecology class and the professor shift to the out-of-doors—to the steep slope that falls off to the south of the farm shop, where a few majestic beech trees define both soil surface and the approach to sky. This class, an elective in the Friends' World program, is full of students each year. Every Monday, during autumn term, we proceed like this—two to three hours of lecture and discussion, with a focus on relevant articles and assigned books, then lunch together featuring farm food freshly harvested (singular in the week of an average college student), then it's out to the fields to thin plants, to cultivate, or to bring in the harvest for the winter share. If we judge by the enthusiasm of these students, experiential learning works.

When we study soils, I always lead the students to the hillside under the towering beech trees. There, under an accumulation of years of leaves, we will find the richest soil on the farm. The drainage is excellent—just enough rainwater, but not too much, will run under the leaf matter to aid in decomposition. This patch of hillside is shady, and basically undisturbed by human footfall. There is an annual assurance of a fresh supply of good carbon material, lightly applied (from above). We are visitors to an Eden for earthworms.

Parting the leaves, the students are amazed at the deep chocolate color of this organic stuff. What we lift into our palms is really a layer of digested material—worm castings—resting halfway between a layer of leaf litter and topsoil, or what we call the earth. These worm castings are not fine-ground, such as silt or clay, but are in aggregate form, with spaces (that's important) within the pill-like structure of this elemental earth. An ideal soil is made up of 45 percent minerals, 5 percent organic matter, and 50 percent space. Space, in this particular agronomic definition, is half air, half water. What we hold in our hands is what the worms have made from the roof of their world—oak and beech leaves, acorns and beech nuts, some bark, and branches from the understory plants. We are told that nature can manufacture an inch of topsoil every seven hundred years; in those terms we are privileged to hold in our hands the gold from under the beech leaves. We hope to encourage similar decomposition in the crop fields—the metamorphosis of organic matter into nutrient-rich soil—so we experiment with cultural practices to mimic the soil in formation on the shady hillside.

Worms moisten the matter they consume with a liquid from their body that contains chemicals to assist digestion. Apparently worms are particular about the leaves they eat; I judge that beech leaves are among their favorites. As worms move through the soil, basically eating their way, they loosen the structure, especially if it is hard-packed. They also serve to combine minerals with the soil particles, and by creating space between soil particles, worms assure that more oxygen will be available for microorganisms and for plant life. The castings we find under the leaves are actually a mixture of this potential soil and of the earth the worms bring up from their burrows. Earthworms are sometimes known as nature's plows.

We have to be careful, when we are the ones who wield the plow, that we do not destroy the essential structure of our soils. We choose to use a chisel plow for tillage, which rakes through the soil, rather than a moldboard plow, which inverts the soil. If we had the time and a thousand extra hands, we would spade over the entire garden. Whatever method is chosen, the gardener or farmer should labor to maintain the crumb structure and, hopefully, to improve it. The object is to aid the process of humification, whereby humus is created, so that the life forces within a soil will be available to plants. We want to encourage the interaction between the living and non-living components within the organic matter of a soil, so that the entire soil ecosystem will function in balance. Worms are masters of this art, and their traffic through the earth is a quiet statement of interdependence.

Hans Jenny comments that when he considers the live weight, estimated by soil biologists, he concludes that there is more biomass under the ground than above it. He speaks of soil itself as a living system. This might make perfect sense to us, but that is because Hans Jenny and others have prepared us for it. When he began thinking in terms of a "larger system," the term "ecosystem" did not exist. He likens natural soils to abstract art, and he claims that "Soil speaks to us through the colors and sculptures of its profile, thereby revealing its personality. . . ."

When I walk with the students from the hillside under the beech trees, where we uncover the castings left by earthworms, to the nearby valley rich in silt loam after years of fallow between two farming enterprises, to Hurricane Hill, where monocropping reduced the liveliness of the loam, they learn to recognize "personality" in soil. The changes we witness on such a walk, and the changes I can see after farming the same ground for fifteen years using ecological techniques, are changes brought about by time; Hans Jenny's (poetic) insights were born out of his ability to link our time and "deep time." The ecological staircase that he studied, located on the coast of California, contains soils formed over half a million years ago. Gazing at a chalky substance, part of the staircase that contains almost no nutrients, and almost no organic matter, he still could exclaim, "Soils are beautiful!"

As I spade up a patch of turf on the hill under a thick mat of clover—for the class to examine—a dark loam teeming with micro and macro life, I agree. This was the poorest part of the field when we started, and now, with the help of compost and legumes, and a respect for the limits of time, we welcome back earthworms, pill bugs, millipedes, springtails, amoebas, molds, and bacteria, and we can witness some health in this soil. I have to be honest—we're building it up to grow some more annual crops, and we want the soil nutrients to impart health to our plants. But I tell the class, as I return the spade full of clover to the mother soil, that I, too, have a deep respect for "deep time," and incessant questions concerning our place in the larger system. And I wonder, with Jenny, "What does nature have in mind in making soils?"

MEADOW MUSIC

For a few weeks now he has been there, singing from some corner of the farm truck. "But what does he eat?" Sarah questions. "Crumbs. And there is no shortage in the Ford," my wife, Megan, replies. So in any weather this cricket keeps us company, and we supply food for song. Lately, to return the favor, I am humming some Cornish melodies, as we travel through the change of seasons.

Perhaps you have not stopped to consider how it is that a cricket sings. My son Liam, who is on familiar terms with autumn insects, informed me one day that he had seen and heard sound rise from the wings of a cricket. I paused—surely they make sound with their legs. I love crickets and the time of year they celebrate, and I have saved many out of the path of foot or wheel or ball, and I have urged them to seek asylum behind the fridge, but have I ever examined the source of song? If you, like me, have doubts, turn to *The Cricket in Times Square*:

> "Chester, make that noise again for Harry," said Tucker Mouse.
>
> Chester lifted the black wings that were carefully folded across his back and with a quick, expert stroke drew the top one over the bottom. A "thrumm" echoed through the station.

"I thought it was singing," said Tucker. "But you do it like playing a violin, with one wing on the other?"

"Yes," said Chester. "These wings aren't much good for flying, but I prefer music anyhow."

After reading this to Liam, before bed, as he casually spooned his yogurt, he responded very matter-of-factly: "See, I told you."

We are also providing other food and living space for cicadas, beetles, and butterflies. As we sow the grains to cover soil we also stimu-

late other harmonies—witness the crickets. In the valley, we leave the wild stands of milkweed for monarchs, who also pause on the white blossoms of buckwheat as a flight school of other pollinators visit the honeysuckle. Our late plantings of greens nourish the autumn insects, and various mustards—arugula, tatsoi, mizuna, and autumn poem—taste as tender as the first spring greens, to us, and them.

Harvesting late peppers, eggplant, and celery in our Town Lane field, I pause to hear a collective insect voice rise out of the sea of clovers, bluestem, and goldenrod.

Crows nestle on the corn stems and cry, a few ride the wind and disappear over the hedgerow. Edgar Wallis, master cliff gardener, could respond to this meadow music with an agile gesture, or a song of his own. It was possible for him, with the flick of an arm, or a token of speech, to act in harmony with his environment, part of the supporting chorus. Preparing a cliff meadow for new potatoes or violets, we worked within a small space bordered by granite rock; some of the walls, built to shelter plants from the sea, rose well above our heads. As we worked with the long-handled cliff shovels, Edgar would spontaneously break into song, timed to the wash of the tide on granite rocks just below us, and above, the pock of jackdaws' wings on currents of air.

Whether in the meadows, or in the village, with every gesture Edgar revealed his connection with living things. A very narrow single-lane road passes through Mousehole, which follows the curve of the harbor. There are a number of blind corners where cars meet and retreat and pause for those on foot. Once, coming around the corner in a narrow spot, on foot, and recognizing Megan and me in our Austin Mini, Edgar proceeded straight ahead to a robust flowering hydrangea, where he opened his arms as if to encircle the globe, and with his eyes still on us, he embraced the plant! As we rolled by, he continued to hug the bush.

By chance, this year we planted Maris Piper, a "tatie" I planted together with Edgar, on the cliff slopes of Cornwall. Tending the plants this season in our peninsular fields of silt loam, walking the rows, an ocean's roar just beyond the dune, I encounter the man. In the voice of the cricket, a diminutive relative surviving on crumbs, I hear an echo of his meadow music.

When he called to me from the Deep Lane field we affectionately refer to as Hurricane Hill, I could not quite distinguish all of the words, but I did hear something in reference to a baby, and then, I thought, "in the valley, by the stand." I was closing up for the night, fastening the fences, moving boxes, papers, and crates back up to the shop. And there, on the wooden bench by the stand I found the answer to Mike M.'s words that had been lost on the wind—mother and tiny child, at one under the apple tree, at peace in the center of the mandala, surrounded by the green of early-autumn hedges, vines, and grasses. When the new papa, Mike, arrived in the valley bearing his harvest, I saw in this threesome "centuries' gift" (my wife's words). In the serenity of the early evening light, and the quietude that surrounds a birth—lasting for weeks and months—the disturbances of the day and of history were overcome by the

essence of field, family, and harvest. It is inherent in the daily function of a community farm to connect land and people; it is a gift to
see the kinship revealed. As Wordsworth wrote, "And then a child
went forth. . . ."

A few weeks ago, mid-September, I received some photographs
via e-mail, of a little garden in Manhattan, surrounded by small
granite blocks. The garden was planted alongside other vegetable
and flower plots, as part of Battery Park's community garden, by
Mike M. I recognized the plants—some summer squash, rows of
mesclun lettuce, and other greens, grown from seeds and transplants I had given Mike a few weeks before. He made a small sign
that proudly said: QUAIL HILL WEST. The sign was gone within a few
days, but no matter—the spirit of the man who sowed the seeds is
strong.

This garden is planted in soil newly transported to the site. In the
background of the photo is the vacant place where once stood the
World Trade Center buildings. For one year, a wreck of vehicles,
stacked twenty-five feet high, took the place of the gardens. Now
the scrap metal is gone, and another kind of industry replaces it: the
industry of humans dedicated to renewal, as the secret source
within each seed is so inclined. Out of the ashes, lettuces. All living
things draw sustenance from the center of the wheel of renewal.
Although we can hold a seed in our palm, pinch the husk and touch
the cellular structure, it is the invisible energy within that ensures
that the wheel revolves. It is the privilege of the gardener to save the
seed, to plant the seed, and to watch the wind carry the invisible life
within forward.

THE SAW-WHET'S WINGS

It is mid-October, the harvest season in Zone 7, and our farm stand, which serves as the information board for community farm members, will be closed in two weeks' time. I was invited, earlier in the year, to attend a Conversation Series at the Murie Center, located in Moose, Wyoming. I have chosen to visit Moose for "Inspiring an effective voice for the Earth," to be held October 14–17 at the former home of Olaus and Mardy Murie, at the base of the Tetons. The timing is perfect. We are midway between cover cropping, to prepare for winter, and the late harvest of roots, which will be stored in the root cellar until March. I will be gone for a week, to the West, to return in time for garlic planting. The soil is prepared to receive the cloves, nourished by an additional layer of compost and gypsum, and we invite sun, rain, and wind to once again initiate another growing bed. We willfully adjust, weather provides.

Before I leave, in order to establish a good cover crop on some erodible land, we harrow the soil to soothe the sloping ground, so that seed will take and water will not run at will. I am still amazed to find how quickly, and with such energy, water will cut or carve a gulley through relatively flat land. Local wisdom (and, indeed, local law) requires that a farmer put down cover crop seed by the fifteenth of October. Then there will be time for the grain seed to establish an adequate network of roots to hold the soil through the winter season.

Olaus and Mardy Murie came to the ranch at the base of the

Tetons in 1945, and Olaus became director of the Wilderness Society. They purchased a seventy-seven-acre piece of river bottom land, formerly the STS Dude Ranch, from their friends Buster and Frances Estes. The Muries had spent many years together in Alaska, which included a honeymoon journey by dogsled into the Koyukuk wilderness. Olaus was employed as a wildlife biologist by the U.S. Biological Survey, and Mardy had been reared in the frontier town of Fairbanks, Alaska Territory. Just after the birth of their first child, Mardy accompanied Olaus on a summer-long boat expedition, in which they often poled their way, inch by inch, into an unchartered landscape. She was not a woman to be left behind.

When I arrived at the camp by the curving Snake River, Mardy was there, under daily care, in her homestead cabin, holding on to her 101 years of life. Although she was spoken of rarely, there was a silent acknowledgment, almost palpable, like the quaking of the last aspen leaves, of her presence. At a seven-thousand-foot elevation it was later in the autumn in Moose than on the Atlantic fishtail island I had left. The woods that surround the cabins were colored by evergreens, not the leaves of aspen and cottonwood, and the nights were crisp and cold. Snow would soon define the landscape, and the Muries had been at home with elk, owl, and marten, in land covered by whiteness.

When I am away from the home farm, land I am drawn down into, my bodily sensations awaken to receive the expressions of an unknown land. At the base of the Teton range the high plateau expands as far as one's eye can see. The mountains, sudden, abrupt, craggy, and commanding, dominate, to be sure. But such a presence also creates a space for a particular animal freedom. In relation to the strict, calculated edifice of solid rock, the high plain is a place to roam. We come to explore or witness, but the animal species that have evolved here are adapted to movement; they participate in the perennial dance of survival, enacted on a wide canvas. At the base of peaks 13,000 feet high I first imagine, and then recognize, the interplay of expansiveness and containment.

We spend the days talking, as the Muries would do, with friends. They were explorers, pioneers at home in wilderness, but they were also family minded; they sought and created community, they were inspiring conversationalists. Because of their work and their vision, they were visited by conservationists, artists, and statesmen as well as by neighbors. When they moved to the ranch, Olaus retired from the Biological Survey, and his vast energy was directed toward wilderness preservation. In 1960, in part because of the Muries' dedication to the Alaskan landscape, the Arctic National Wildlife Refuge was created. After Olaus died, in 1963, Mardy was present at the signing of the Wilderness Act by Lyndon Johnson (she received a pen). And her tireless efforts helped to create the Alaska National Interest Lands Conservation Act, which protected 104 million acres of land, signed into being by Jimmy Carter. The Muries were great defenders of wilderness, and Mardy has been called the mother of American conservation. The Murie Center came into being for the sake of "the wild human spirit," to explore the value of nature and of wild places, and to expand and strengthen the conservation community.

As I walk away from the expanse of the plain, into the dense woodlands, toward the beaver ponds, my mind returns to certain open fields at sea level. As I walk through the cottonwoods and as-pen of Wyoming, very much present, I can also see the fluted bark of beech and the smooth oaks that surround our farm fields. Daily, during the growing season, I plan and negotiate a patterned land-scape. We seed and transplant into rows, I traverse the rows on foot or machine, and turn to address the next row. The cover crops I re-cently seeded can be seen from above as a green postage stamp. And the fences we erect, literally miles of electrical strand, are meant to keep out visitors from the wild. But I am still conscious of the wild culture of the land, and I can wonder at it in my palm. It has been said that the undiscovered country lies immediately below us, in the soil—and in what is living there, in a fistful of it, or in the acres of loam that may support a field of oats or wheat, we may also discover the ground, the basis of wilderness. When we turn the soil for our practical purpose, with a spade or chisel plow, we fill it with air. When we add organic matter to create humus and improve tilth, we prepare the path for water, we interact with the elements. The spirit of the soil is wild with microbial life.

"Wait, don't move, look, ahead, on the fallen tree," whispers Virginia, my trail companion. Virginia is here from the Mad River valley of Vermont and the Vermont Land Trust; she has been instrumental not only in preserving property, but in raising questions concerning the interplay of land, ethics, and human feelings. Her eyes are open in the woods.

"See, under that tangle of branches, it's a weasel, or maybe a marten."

I do see it, a low, sleek form moving with speed along the horizontal log, dipping into and under branches, diving from view. It has a rich, full coat, the color of late autumn grasses drying in a meadow. Neither Virginia nor I had ever seen such a creature, and it did not linger to satisfy our curiosity. We saw it as a messenger of this rugged landscape—a beautiful, wild form, tangible and elusive at once. Later, when we reported our sighting to those who knew these woods, we learned that Mardy's favorite creature was a pine marten. But the colors of the creature we saw did not match those of a marten; could it be a fisher? But a fisher is very rarely seen, even by those who know where to look. Were we sure that the tail was really that long, that the coat was a soft brown? Virginia and I nodded at each other, secure with our story, content with the small mystery, the direct communication from the Moose woods.

After our meeting with that sleek mammal we make our way along the trail that widens out to some wetlands, the beaver ponds, with rough, massive peaks rising beyond. There we divide, in search of silence, Virginia to a sunny meadow just through the shallow water, and I to continue up the trail along the water's edge. A fine wind is blowing, causing the tops of firs to sway against the brilliant blue above points of stone. I am alone with the mountain wind, the sound of slow moving water, the raucous cry of a crow, and with my notebook.

The poet Ezra Pound wrote: "Do not move / Let the wind speak. . . ." Here, it is filled with the mineral breath of Teton rock. As I lean back against a tall fir, I am joined by chickadees and nuthatches who dip from the low branches, their precise wings percussive as they dive. The slow, repetitive brush of a branch against a sapling accompanies the songbirds and the wind in the higher trees. In this landscape the musical variations are infinite. And the conversations of wood on wood, water over stone, feather to bone, I hope will inform my own.

When I return to the trail, after contemplation at the edge of the woods, I pass the homestead cabin where Mardy, too, is at rest. I know she is there, 101 years of age, at the wilderness line of life, and her legacy, embodied in spirit of place, reflects like sunlight on cottonwood, on balsam fir, and on the wings of an eagle high over the Snake.

Toward the end of the day we all decide to hike out to a certain mountain meadow, a place where the elk (also known as wapiti) are known to gather. We hope to get a good view of a band of them from the shelter of the trees, and to hear some bugling.

Sure enough, the wapiti arrive in the open field, at the base of the Teton range, shortly after we do. We move to the edge of the tree line, still a thousand feet from the band of elk, though with binoculars they are easy to study. They are restless, feeding and moving throughout the field. The huge, dominant bull, possessive of his harem, at times breaks into a run to chase off one of the younger males who linger just outside the invisible circle of demarcation. They sense our presence, or detect a movement, and they scatter into the far woods. When they return the bull's bugling echoes over the land, a haunting song, the sound amplified by the backdrop of rock. We watch as a young bull, in ritual fashion, approaches his dominant elder. They each lower their substantial rack of antlers to touch the ground, their heads bowed to the earth. When their antlers touch they rattle their heads from side to side, and the clatter and clack of bone nearly shakes the ground. After the test, the bold teenager backs away from the harem, and the number-one bull lifts his stately rack to fill the air with deep bugling.

Meanwhile, another conversation is beginning. I hear a sound behind me, and when I turn I find four or five of our party facing away from the elk, standing, in silence, before a spruce, looking up. Curious, I join the shadowy figures beneath the tree, and when my eyes adjust to the darkness, I can just detect another inhabitant of this high country. There, on a branch, six feet above the ground, an alert saw-whet owl has found the perfect perch to investigate us. Someone had heard the particular "chirp-chirp" of the saw-whet as the tiny raptor rushed past us into the spruce. Fellow travelers in the dusk, we face eye to eye, outside of time, before the small, curious owl darts away into the darker woods. Our contact was specific and direct, informed by the precise architecture of feathers, and the clarity of mountain air.

Walking back to the cabins, I found myself beside Nancy Shea, director of the Murie Center, and I thought it was time to tell her about the poem, insistent in my mind, suggested by a recurrent theme of the day. That morning, as I was ready to read the words, our conversation swerved in another direction. This poem, which I wrote years before, after a personal loss, describes a scene in the quiet of a Zen meditation room in which Peter Matthiessen, also a friend of the Muries, lifts a small, lifeless bird out of the folds of his robes, after thirty minutes of sitting in silence. The owl had hit a window, and Peter, hoping to revive it, laid it against his chest: "Then the surprise gift of death: / the saw-whet's wings / in the teacher's hands / taken from his black robes. . . ."

That bright night, among the firs at the base of the Teton range, I was face to beak with what a friend calls "the miracle of the realness," here revealed by a small raptor and the music of words.

Later, I remembered a passage from John Hay: "We become more than we are when there are others than ourselves, whether of foreign speech, or no speech at all, to measure our lives by. . . . This new country, this older wilderness that spawned us, exists by reason of the inclusion of infinite force, danger, and opportunity. The only reality is in participation."

The following morning I was awoken very early by the natural music of the Wyoming landscape. First, the slow, continuous "who-who, who-who-who-who" of an owl, high in the trees beside my cabin. When I crept out to see, I was greeted by the sound of several elk, far off in the woods by the beaver ponds, not proud bugling, but a sound as soothing as a nursery melody played by a number of flutes to welcome in the morning.

Mardy Murie wrote, "Who knows what is ahead in the long march of evolution? But saving the last remnants of wild, untouched country seems to me to be the one wise, altruistic, beneficial, and practical action this nation can take for its sanity."

On the nineteenth of October, three days after the saw-whet awakened us at dusk, Mardy Murie, who made her home open to all, who spoke with eloquence in quiet places and before the U.S. Congress, who eventually received the Presidential Medal of Freedom, the woman with a passion for wild places and wild creatures, died peacefully in her cabin in the Moose woods. When I heard the news I also heard, with equal clarity, the quick voice of the saw-whet. I hear still the rasp of feather and bone as the bird, leaving the spruce, wings home.

TO PROVIDE SOME HARMONY

At soil level, cheek against clover, I see the green stems of garlic—*Allium sativum ophioscorodon*—like sail masts over the sea of mulch. Planted five weeks ago, the clove roots are firm, resolute, in the rich Amagansett ground, holding onto the perfect mixture of clay, sand, and silt that gives us loam. Under this layer of alfalfa, the garlic cloves settle into winter and send up a stalk to reach for the light.

Eight weeks ago we spread our compost over the garlic growing bed, disced it into the soil, prepared the bed for planting. Twelve weeks ago, we tilled in the cover mixture of clover that we sowed in spring to oversummer. The summer before we planted beans to harvest, and to enrich the soil. The summer before that, compost, lime, carrots, and a cover crop of rye and vetch. Each year the soil tilth improves as we trust the natural thrust toward diversity.

A neighbor pointed out to me, "Before you began farming here, this was just an eroded hillside." For fifteen years, we've tilled and disced and moved soil, but we have also planted grains and legumes to return fertility, we've rested land, rotated crops, studied the contours. We have changed from a garden prepared with a hand-pushed rototiller to a small farm with five tractors in use (limited, in the case of the '48 Ford and the '52 Massey Harris). Although I still direct seed with my $65 Earthway Special, the scale of plantings and plants and people in the field has changed significantly. We've changed, but why are we here, and farming? I'm fond of the grand questions, following in the mode of Wendell Berry, who entitled a book *What Are People For?*

Cheek against clover, near to the *sativum,* I am better able to reflect. We are here to provide a local source of organic food through the practice of sustainable agriculture. We are here to take care of a piece of earth, some local soil, to preserve and enrich what is called "prime agricultural soil." We are here to create and renew daily conversations, among children of all ages, against the backdrop of a mature apple tree, a wave of sunflowers, rows of garlic stems rising out of straw. And we're here to continue to question—as we build a healthy soil on a small island blessed with glacial deposits—who discovers the richness? As we preserve and protect more land and open space, who is it for? As we admire the harvest and create a community, can we also begin to build a new commons?

In *The Great Remembering* Peter Forbes writes,

> Those who believe that land conservation can build a new commons for land and people have a different story to tell Americans. In this story, we do not surrender fully to a culture defined by self-preservation, the abhorrence of limits, and the expectation of rewards. We create, instead, an expanded parable of land conservation, a story that breathes life into a community-based culture defined by mutual interdependence, a belief in limits, and a love of service. This story doesn't naively suggest that a relationship to land and nature is the whole answer to all our social pathologies, but it offers it as a first answer. Land is the foundation of our cultural house. Our relationship to the land and our ability to listen to its story— one infinitely larger than our own—are defining choices in who we will become.

I remember musing on these questions in another autumn, as I paddled a backwater creek north of Savannah, Georgia. I had just attended a seminar for land conservationists entitled "Why Are We Here?" I watched a young bald eagle circle above the Tupelo as a white heron stalked in shallow water, dwarfed by the huge buttressed bases of the cypresses. According to the guide, because of a long drought, the Ebenezer Creek was at least eight feet lower than he had ever seen it. The backwater woods are dark and deep, and some of the cypresses are one thousand years old. Now the base of the buttress, usually submerged in dark water, was revealed, in tree after tree. Moving down the river we looked into the oval mouth of each cypress, waiting for a word to emerge. Above, small birds were in flight among the moss. As the canoe approached, a few yellow-bellied sliders (turtles) left their rocks in the sun to smooth into the brown water. It was not difficult to hear in these wet woods sounds of the ages drifting through the hanging moss to be swallowed into the wooden caverns of the swamp trees.

Floating on a creek in such an elemental landscape, or bedding down in straw to investigate garlic, I am influenced by the late autumn mood. Looking up, from the gentle curves of the Long Island topography, I see flocks of starlings alter the sky. Like a singular flash across the surface of the sea, a moving swell of birds punctuates the diminishing day. And when a flock descends to the beech trees, the melody they make is accompanied by the percussive fall of nuts and husks. We call this open space—a place we are able to walk and listen to the movements of birds, to drift by boat and witness the resonant hollows of cypresses. In this open space we can still take care to preserve the music we want to hear, we can still be surprised by hawk or redwing, eagle or slider, rufous-sided towhee, or blister beetle. The music we make at Quail Hill Farm is voiced by the leaves of chard, cauliflower, and calliopsis, the roots of buckwheat, clover, and bellbeans, the garlic cloves bedded under alfalfa straw. Why are we here? We are here to provide some harmony.

Last night, lying between my daughter and son on their nightly journey into sleep, I listened to the autumn insects in the oaks. The textures came alive—leaves like shadows drifting onto dark water, the movement of wings through moss or leaves, squirrels traveling across rough bark and trusting the upper branches. All of this sensory material I measure as a home seed sound—this is sense of place. I also hear, distant in space, but distinct, the beat of wings above a creek, the sharp sound of nuts hitting the backwater. It is possible to replace the abstract question—why are we here?—with a local knowledge. With such knowledge, when a turtle's belly touches water we share her sense of stone, tupelo, backwater. When a starling touches down to beech limb we share her sense of autumn air, the cool darkness descending. And it is possible to pause with the heron at water's edge, and to hear, before we pass by, within the ages of wood, and sustaining, the home seed sound.

"THE SWEET INFLUENCES
OF THE PLEIADES"

After a day of rain, I stepped out last night to address the open sky full of sparkles. At this time of autumn, looking south to the ocean, I encounter the belt of Orion, just climbing the horizon, pointed up toward the cluster of the Pleiades. On such a night, after a good season, a single line occurs to me out of the clarity of memory, accompanied by an ordinary stream of gardener's thoughts: "The night is clear and cold . . . so the carrots are sweetening in the soil . . . after the rainfall the newly planted garlic will start to send out roots . . . will the greenhouse lettuce seeds sprout as quickly in the cold?" And on, for a time, as I am gazing into the blazing night mirror.

So we leave the carrots—taking a chance—until we hear the hard frosts are coming; then it will be time to dig and cart carrots into the root cellar. Today, having heard that the night temperature could drop into the twenties, we called on all available hands to bring in some of the crops. A portion of the potatoes is boxed and stored in our root cellar already, as well as a portion of the beet, rutabaga, and black radish crops. In the main room of the farm shop, drier yet still cool, we've stored delicata, sweet dumpling, butternut squash, and onions, and this summer's garlic, tied in bunches, floats above it all. Still in the soil, and growing sweeter— cabbages, celeriac, and leeks. When we catch notice of the next freeze we will dig parsnips and burdock root, crops that can, on certain years, overwinter in the field. Burdock root, the most tenacious vegetable on the planet, also collects the prize for "earthiness" in any test of taste. One year, a farm member who had settled here from Japan brought me a memorable thank-you dinner of burdock, carrots, scallions, garlic, and shoyu, sprinkled with sesame seeds. This was a more than adequate reward for forking deep into our silt loam for the long roots of this earthy, sweet vegetable, a staple of the macrobiotic diet.

We often leave cabbages in the field until Christmas, which is a bonus of raising vegetables in Zone 7. These tightly wrapped members of the brassica family can weather some hard frosts, and frost improves their taste. I learned to grow brassicas in the home of cabbages and kings, the West Country of England. In Cornwall brassica transplants—broccoli, cabbage, sprouts—could be purchased at the local greengrocer shop. There they were, lying in a dry bin, in bunches, twenty-five spindly stalks sprouting a few random leaves, bound together by a rubber band. When I first learned of this custom, I could not recognize these slender stalks as living plants. With a guarantee from the grocer I carried the transplants home, stuck them deep in the soil of the meadows, and waited for rain. For a few days the cabbages keeled over, heated by a rare display of sun, and then, after the first hour of rainfall (the wait is generally not long), the stalks stood up and made an effort to sprout new leaves. Several rains and months later each slender stalk fattened to a globe weighing five pounds or more.

Still, I had no idea how hearty these plants could be until last year's crop withstood a week of frigid temperatures. Caught by surprise, I assumed I had lost the crop; when I split one in two it was frozen solid, as if it had been placed in the deep freeze. One week later, after a thaw, I went to inspect; the cabbages were fine, seemingly unaffected by the freeze. We harvested in the last week of December, and they stored for three months in the root cellar.

This year our autumn crop of brassicas has been saved by a light-weight black plastic netting borrowed from a local vineyard. The spring crop, planted in a back field, far from human traffic, was claimed by the crows. I have been hesitant to accept that this is now their field. I was understanding when they feasted on our corn, one of their favorite foods, and I accepted the loss of the ripest tomatoes. I admit that I was very surprised when they attacked a crop of capsicum, peppering the fruit with their sharp beaks. Do they really care for green peppers? Well, they do care for cabbages; before we could harvest the tender spring crop the crows removed the hearts of 1,500 heads. They kindly left the robust stalks for the gardeners.

The vineyard covering is working, for the time being; the crows seem hesitant to catch their toes in the netting, even in search of cabbage. I'm worried when I see a caucus of crows in the sassafras trees, beside the field crops. Their sound does not resemble idle conversation; the debate, I'm sure, is how to negotiate netting.

A few weeks ago, while digging the sweet potatoes—or attempting to at least—I remarked to the crew: "This is one good reason why I continue to farm." The impulse is connected quite directly to holding the fruits of one's labor in one's hands. It is also connected with another sentiment: "How in the world do I get this done?"

Each new task demands a fresh solution, while the same task in another year requires another solution. We were quite surprised this year, on our first attempt, with our abundant harvest of sweet potatoes. They grew to be so fat, due to abundance of rain, that our antique potato digger succeeded only in cutting the tubers during the harvest. When I lowered the digger, the shovel, or scoop, took in such a weight of soil that the wheels locked—man and machine could not move a yard forward. Determined to preserve the best of this precious crop, more commonly grown in the South, we abandoned the machinery approach and proceeded with forks. Alas, we only continued to cut the tubers. Finally, simply, and rightly so, we tried the trusty shovel, inserted at a specific angle. Up they came, neither bruised nor cut, the sweet evidence of autumn. Hand harvesting on a community farm is a viable option—many hands can usually be found, at least for the promise of sweetness.

I am elated with the robust size and the autumn color of the sweet potatoes, and I am impressed with the flavor, but I was unprepared for the beauty of the flower. These hearty tubers do not derive from the same family—nightshades—as our more familiar spuds. Sweet potatoes, *Ipomoea batatas,* are a member of the Convolvulaceae family—like morning glories, they are vines. We kept them well weeded, and let them travel—a few vines ran over fifteen feet. They proved to be the favorite food of deer (have I said this of another vegetable?), so we disguised the vines by sowing buckwheat throughout the plants. Sometime in September, three months after planting the sweet potato slips, a ray of sun happened upon one white bell-shaped flower, lighting the ruby center. Surprised by the flower in early autumn, I paused in the field to welcome a new cultivar to the good loam of Amagansett.

So last night, when I stepped out to observe the sky, taking in a breath of cool autumn air, this is the remembered line (recalling William Blake's illustrations to the Book of Job):

> Can'st thou bind the sweet influences of the Pleiades, or
> loose the bands of Orion?

As if in acknowledgment, certainly in response, following my words by a second, in the clarity of the southern sky I saw a rush of light. A shooting star flashed under the Pleiades and disappeared into the belt of Orion. This gardener's thoughts, near the close of a season, are filled with the sparks of stars.

"THE ATMOSPHERE
I WANTED TO BE IN"

Last night our fields felt the first light touch of Jack Frost, his earliest visit in my years of farming here. Some of the leaves of the brassicas were touched, some of the thin-skinned pumpkins, and some basil, usually the first to go; we are trusting that thousands of winter squash that are curing in our field will shake off the frost and continue to sweeten. Several years ago, knowing that our storage squash could survive a light frost, we took a chance. That night the temperature fell down into the mid-twenties, and the entire crop of butternuts, the finest storage squash, was decorated with a thin white covering of frost. We harvested the butternuts, and they were intact, except that each one wore a discolored patch on the shoulders. Two weeks later, long before Thanksgiving, the squash turned soft precisely there, and that signaled the shortest squash storage season on record.

Walking the fields I note the abundant growth of our cover crops—oats and bellbeans or field peas—fed by days of autumn rain that washed a soil still warm. As we bend to harvest the crops that still produce some fruit, we attempt to step lightly on the clover, seed sown under the existing crop (the technique is appropriately known as undersowing) weeks ago, now surfacing as a grass cover to hold the soil over the winter season. These grains and legumes and grasses will feed our silt loam with increased organic matter, the foundation of fertility. Grasses have been called "the forgiveness of nature."

We're still working in the garden at the back of Nick and Toni's, a nearby restaurant, long a supporter of sustainable, local agriculture. Jeff Salaway (Nick), with Toni Ross, attended a gardening workshop I led many years ago at a local school. For ten years Jeff and I were brothers-in-the-field of organic growing. At his request we established a small but productive vegetable garden on a waste lot behind the restaurant. On my first visit to the sad sand lot, on a tractor equipped with a robust rototiller implement, after only a few passes I had successfully ruined the tiller on camouflaged building rubble. We encouraged each other, we heaved out the rubble, the tiller was repaired, we trucked in tons of compost, and I continued to build a garden. After ten years of removing bricks, pipe, and electrical conduit, and yearly adding tons of compost, the garden at Nick and Toni's, planted by the same farmers (us), using the same seed and transplants and methodology, often produces earlier and more abundantly than our plantings in the beautiful silt loam at Quail Hill. I hesitate to mention this—but often the vegetables planted in the sand lot taste better! I use this project as a teaching tool for apprentices, but I am unable to adequately explain the results. I will venture a guess, though—shelter from ocean winds, concentrations of compost, extra loving care.

We grow the plants for the restaurant's garden, informed by weekly meetings in the field of farmer and chefs. We tend the plants, enrich the garden, add straw mulch to the asparagus and tomatoes; the kitchen staff comes out to harvest, and the harvest is served that very evening. After Jeff's tragic death a few years ago, we continue the experiment. The garden is still informed by our original conversations, and these ranged from a discussion of the current crop of Sungolds, to the impressive early growth of asparagus ferns, to the freshest book that must be read (our favorite, *The Botany of Desire*, by Michael Pollan), to a crystal-clear comment by Willem de Kooning: "I got into painting the atmosphere I wanted to be in. It was like the reflection of light. I reflected upon the reflections on the water, like fishermen do."

Our relationship with the restaurant, and all who work there, is supportive and familial, a healthy alternative within the stark reality of the wholesale market. It is this kind of sustained partnership that is essential to the survival of small farms, and to educating those who come to the table. Jeff, informed by a heart and mind impish and curious, reflective and refined, realized the natural link between our rich soils (including the rich soil of one man-made garden) and those who sample a cuisine prepared from those soils. He and those who have followed understand that we are fed by plants continuously—we are fed the gift of possibility.

The beechnuts are falling all around as I write, October music supplied by the energetic grackles. The shadows that inform this woodland space reflect changing colors, colors drifting lightly today after a night's rain. The beeches that surround our farmshop, rare on this island, are majestic with or without leaves. Their smooth, graceful gray bark is compared by all to an elephant's hide—the resemblance is compounded, I believe, by the solid stature of the beeches, the way that they stand upon the earth. Their great limbs reach upward and out, a strong dancer's arms forming a U, and they dwarf the dogwoods and hollies that live under the canopy. In speaking of E. F. Schumacher, Wes Jackson comments that the author of Small Is Beautiful "was a strong advocate of planting and caring for trees which he saw as more than bearers of fruit, for he saw them as symbols of what he called 'permanence,' which he used as a synonym for sustainability." One of these symbols of permanence, wide enough at the base that two men can just touch fingers when hugging the beech, stands at the entrance to our farm building, touching the fascia board, and sending its great branches upward to produce an umbrella of leaves over our roof. The hens are out today under the beech, happily flipping leaves and nuts, exposing another world of insects, and adding to the chorus of grackles.

As I watch the hurried movement of squirrels and chipmunks

under the canopy of oaks and through the autumn grasses, I am reminded of a certain summer day when the Quail Hill crew gathered to admire a colony of hoptoads, leaping toward the safety of the raspberries. Preparing the ground for a cover crop, by tractor, I had disturbed their home in the field. Luckily, they are tiny enough and quick enough to escape the blade of the harrow, the traffic of the tractor. We assisted their hopping. Each year I am aware of more life supported by our soil, from microbial life to earthworm to hoptoad. Apparently these creatures respond to our farming methods. This is a lesser-known achievement of organic farming—as soil health improves in a managed field, more wildlife (all sizes and dimensions) can return. Whatever it is we may provide for them, the hoptoads give back to us with each tiny, ridiculous, and lovely leap.

Fascinated by the movement of toads in the field, we have also noted the various traffic this year of deer, crows, pheasants, and field mice. Our vegetable crops seem to intersect with their chosen movements, so as we provide food for our farm members, we also provide for local wildlife. In a gesture of friendship, we are determined to grow more. Taking the sprightly attitude of the toads at season's end, we hope to continue this conversation that occurs between common ground and sky, and to harvest our share of the fruits, the good product of fine soils, labor, luck, rain, and sun.

WINTER

Then waxwings snip the wick of day
supper's good and wood is dry,
headboard's hum as freight goes by.
Next morning, up and back,
every fencepost wears a cap.

—MILTON KESSLER,
"WAXWINGS," 1990

RIBBON, STONE, SHELL,
AND BONE

The black lettering on the white sign in the valley states clearly: Kale & Collard Greens, Please Harvest the Larger, Outside Leaves. I have encountered an icy problem, however; rows of pale green plants still evident, but encased in what is now a frozen lake, reaching over the greens to the raspberries in the valley. On a wet, cold, real winter day such as this, the center of the apple orchard is transformed into a smooth skating pond. I was amazed to find, when I climbed onto the frozen pile of oak leaves we composted this autumn, that only twelve inches down the microbes were at work—enough heat rose to warm my hands. This almost invisible form of life feeds on what we call waste and decay, turning the raw materials into humus, generating heat within a space surrounded by ice. This essential, transformative work takes place beneath our gaze, as we focus on snow crystals descending or a sheet of ice illumined by the low winter sun.

A few weeks ago, before the freeze, as I was passing our fields on Town Lane, a small shape in the center of the field, moving slightly in the wind, caught my eye. Whatever it was, impossible to tell from a distance, this animal or object was stationary, yet moving with the wind, something that the eye sees instantly, like the wing beat of a heron over a hedge, a small shape prominent in the middle of a sea of green winter rye. My curiosity only increased as I approached, still unable to discern—whose feathers? Why are those legs so stiff?

Only when I waded into the middle of the field of rye did I

recognize the inanimate object with such "presence," placed there, I now realized, by Paul H., to bless the field. Feathers tipped in the breeze, small stones wrapped in yarn, bone and shell were spinning around a curved oak branch planted in winter soil—it was a prayer stick. We had made ornaments with the children at the winter solstice, a custom once practiced by Native Americans on the shortest day—they planted prayer sticks in the field to ensure the return of light and fertility. Singular in a sea of green, made by careful hands weaving ribbon, stone, shell, and bone, this oak stick carried the sound of centuries and the quietude of a man's footsteps on winter grass.

The ornament—or prayer—in the rye defined this place with a fine eloquence. Immediately, I was able to see the winter soil, the tangled hedge, the sassafras trees, the volunteer cedars, the lone bare birch, with greater clarity. What is it that is meant by the words "spirit of place"? We certainly mean to describe a physical setting— a field, a valley, a row of trees, a pond—but can we agree on what spirit is? If we consult esoteric tradition, the conversation could be endless, and lead to abstraction. Shakespeare's words are clear enough, spoken in *The Tempest* by Prospero, the magician who chooses to bury his staff "certain fathoms in the earth": "These our actors / As I foretold you, were all spirits and / Are melted into air, into thin air. . . ." The substantial fabric of Prospero's island is animated with what is invisible. And the spirit of place, here on this farm, is influenced by insistent, colorful lichen clinging to oak bark, and by the insect life that dwells between bark and heartwood.

David Abram, in *The Spell of the Sensuous*, points out that "a great many terms that now refer to the air as a purely passive and insensate medium are clearly derived from words that once identified the air with life and awareness." He also writes that "the word 'spirit' itself, despite all of its incorporeal and non-sensuous connotations, is directly related to the very bodily term 'respiration' through their common root in the Latin word spiritus, which signified both 'breath' and 'wind.'"

Eugenio Montale, praising the sunflower (here in translation), asks to be brought the plant that transports one to "where the blond hazes shimmering rise / and life fumes to air as spirit does. . . ." Imagine what a sunflower says, or a field of them—stalk, petals, and seeds—and it is possible to have a clearer notion of spirit. It is that which is unseen, but can be sensed in the respiration manifest in rows of *Helianthus*, a thick stand of orchard grass, an elegant beech tree, a trickle of rainwater over stone, an oak branch marking a field.

A gardener, a farmer, a family attentive to the spirit of a place become part of that place when it is viewed not as a commodity but, as Aldo Leopold wrote, as a community to which we belong. Although I am daily engaged in altering a landscape, I hope to listen for the deeper resonance of the place, the spoken words of roots, clay, rock, and aquifer below. The prime soils of Quail Hill prove to be productive as farmland, though the landscape can also serve as sanctuary.

Since my days as an apprentice gardener in England, when I first discovered cosmos, my autumn garden has been colored with the magenta, white, and pink petals of Sea Shells and Picotee. Responding to the rich silt loam at the base of Quail Hill, one planting of cosmos, two rows stretching over 250 feet, soared to a height of seven feet, and the blossoms, encouraged by cutting, kept coming. There was a graceful curve at the far end of the rows, where the tractor was forced to skirt an apple tree, so this chorus of cosmos simulated a wave. On that particular autumn, following the attack on September 11, I remember watching a couple who had just arrived on the South Fork from Manhattan. They wandered toward the flowers with purpose, to cut some stems, but then something took them over, and they became immersed in the cosmos—in a literal and figurative sense—entwined in the silver and green foliage of this now-healing hedge. The gesture of the hedge of cosmos, and their response, was a celebration of the interdependence of seed, life within the soil, and human hands.

Aldo Leopold wrote, "The biota is beautiful collectively and in all its parts. . . . The true problem of agriculture, and all other land use, is to achieve both utility and beauty, and thus permanence. A farmer has the same obligation to help, within reason, to preserve the biotic integrity of his community as he has, within reason, to preserve the culture which rests on it."

A few days after I encountered the prayer stick in the field of rye, snow arrived. The oak woods are still a dream of whiteness, branches heavy and sculpted with wet snow, a dense symphony of drift and fall, delicate dance of bark and flake, a forest of intricate acceptance. I have a photograph of the colorful branch, planted in the green field—a branch decorated by children's hands out of bone, yarn, shell, and feather, and planted at the winter solstice to ensure fertility in the coming year. Today that field is a sea of white. Under the blanket the solstice charm survives. And look, along the hedgerow, up and back, "Every fencepost wears a cap."

FLASHES OF ICE AND CARBON

Pausing in the farm fields at this time of year, when the light, especially at the close of the abbreviated day, illumines the field and hedgerow with a silver fire—as if from a child's reverie, or out of some ancient memory—I am engaged by the seasonal renewal. Looking up, while digging parsnips out of the muckish soil, Matt C. and myself watched vees of geese cover the sky with determined flight and their Nordic symphony. Groups of birds, as if directed, point to the east, then veer to the south, then reverse to the north, breaking off from one formation, then joining another, creating a patternless pattern. After some moments of attention to the ballet in the sky, we redirected our focus, and our digging forks, to the deep roots held by Amagansett loam. Planted by seed in early May, and tended over three seasons, these parsnips will keep in our moist root cellar until March. The melting of snow has softened the ground so that soil slides with ease from the wet roots.

We do not have many customers clamoring for parsnips, but our informal community farm policy dictates that if at least three persons request a specific vegetable, or herb, or flower, we will plant it. There are still more than a few vegetable lovers—not especially young ones—who adore the sweetness of roasted parsnips in the middle of winter. We are lucky to have this crop; it is all too easy to lose track of the seeds, slow to germinate in the month of May. It can be three weeks before the slender leaf shoot appears—and you have to be on your stomach to witness it—so that, if the ground is not quite clean, any variety of weeds will dominate the row. More than once I have forgotten to check the parsnip patch, only to find a very successful row of mixed weeds (the original "mesclun"), enhanced by a few parsnip roots. Taking into account the necessity of thinning—the roots will not mature to a good size without it—and remembering that forty-nine other crops probably need tending, I am apt to hop on the Case, attach a disc harrow, prepare to drag it, and mutter, "Parsnips next year!" Although I consider myself among those who appreciate *Pastinaca sativa*, 120 days to maturity is indeed a long time.

With our thoughts on mulch for the garlic crop, we have waited for the beeches and oaks of Quail Hill to surrender their leaves. They were piled into great mounds down in a hollow off Deep Lane; and then the snow came. When the days began to warm we shredded the leaves with a mower, loaded them into our manure spreader, and transported the potential mulch to the garlic beds in another field. When I engaged the PTO (power take-off) of the tractor to empty the leaves, and the metal beaters began to spin, the air came alive with a diamond spray of snow, ice, oak bark and leaves, and stems of beech. Because of the lowered path of sunlight, even the ordinary transport of leaves became a brilliant symbol of renewal—abstract flashes of ice and carbon to cover an autumn planting of cloves, through winter, until the harvest in the following July.

All throughout the month of December the oats and bellbeans continue to grow, seeds forming on the tall oat stems, clacking in the early winter wind. This can happen during a warm autumn— grains planted as a cover crop, to hold the soil over the winter, actually can mature to seed before the arrival of hard, hard frosts. As December draws to a close, with the help of a number of volunteers (part of the ground, the basis of this farm) we are harvesting carrots, beets, turnips, and cabbage for the root cellar; kale still survives in the field, shaking off the night's ice in the midday sun. The oat stems are still standing up, though the seed music has changed to a rasp, a grain's rattle, when shaken by the north wind.

I began the year, before the fever of tilling, planting, and cultivating, by reading the Earth Charter, a meditative document over ten years in the making. Recently I staged a reading of the charter at a local school, and I asked several students, ranging in age from twelve to eighteen, to join me in reading from a passage that spoke to them. I followed the reading of each part with a poem, by Rumi, C. P. Cavafy, or W. B. Yeats. The preamble contains this: "The resilience of the community of life and the well-being of humanity depend upon preserving a healthy biosphere with all its ecological systems, a rich variety of plants and animals, fertile soils, pure waters, and clean air."

The language is succinct and beautiful, like leaves of grass covered with morning frost, illumined by a winter sun: "I.a. Recognize that all beings are interdependent and every form of life has value regardless of its worth to human beings. 4.b. Transmit to future generations values, traditions, and institutions that support the long-term flourishing of Earth's human and ecological communities. 7. Adopt patterns of production, consumption, and reproduction that safeguard Earth's regenerative capacities, human rights, and community well-being." I can hear the gentle music of this document, pragmatic and timely, as we close the year, and as we dig the last of the carrots from under the straw, and shake the frost off the solid cabbage, ready to be packed into the cellar.

On the last day of the year I'm here at my desk, looking up to the tangled gray boughs of oak, and the deep green, sharp leaves of American holly. My left leg is encased in a cast up to my knee, to keep a fractured ankle immobile for a month, the result of a slight misstep at the close of a satisfying season. So in this forced rest I hope to enjoy the pleasures of my desk, piled high with a fine new edition of Rainer Maria Rilke, and *A Place in Space*, *The Traveler's Tree*, *The Names of Things*, and *The Mind of Clover*. As wind whips the dry oak leaves outside, I open my copy of Rilke to ". . . live my life in widening rings / which spread over earth and sky" and to listen for "Lalage, the Muse, the sound all of nature makes, the language of birds."

And once more, before the time comes to mix the new year's first batch of seed-starting soil, my thoughts return to the farm crew. One really needs to watch them daily to fully appreciate their abilities—from precise seeding, to rough mechanics, to vigilant weeding, usually accomplished with wit and humor. Comfortable with a degree of chaos, I bow to the persistent attempts of Dana K. and Sarah S. to create some temporary order.

Most of our apprentices, the community farm crew, are here for a year to learn, and to absorb some salt spray, and then they move on, to cultivate other gardens. On occasion, when the favorable winds are blowing, we can capture a young person at the impressionable age, for a few years. Sarah S., after three years at Quail Hill, will leave to join the crew of Roxbury Farm in the Hudson valley. I remember meeting her at the bus, as she arrived fresh from Manhattan for interview day: nineteen, shy and tentative, with a mind fine-tuned by literature and the Big Apple. She wore jeans and a brand-new pair of Timberline work boots; she was ready to stir up some dirt.

I will miss her competence combined with a casual air, her kindness, her willingness to tackle a difficult three-point hitch, or to locate the last bit of information I had lost on the Mac. Over three years she learned to plan for crops, to plant and cultivate, to debate with weeds and workers, to make signs for the masses, to master Saturday morning greetings, and to read the changeable weather of Amagansett. We gave her the space to improve her juggling, to learn the ins-and-outs of Case tractors, to hone her judgments concerning capital / land / conservation, and space to construct a fine sukkah. I'm sure that she is the only aspiring organic farmer under the age of forty able to quote several lines from "Binsey Poplars," by Gerard Manley Hopkins. It was my good fortune to have passed the place of those poplars every day for a year, on my bicycle ride to and from Boar's Hill, Oxford, England. So it was our fortune, Sarah's and mine, to share the poem and a passion for words and the soil. We often caught each "morning morning's minion," whether looking for the red-tailed hawk (the windhover), the first fresh shoots of asparagus, or steam rising from straw at the nascent end of the compost row. Sarah would appreciate the Latinate word, and also the basic meaning of the matter—compost improves field fertility. She pinned these words—from Lynn Miller—above her desk in the farm shop: "Keep it small, go slow, take care, and mix it up." In my rush to consider the day's charming chaos, and to intuit "mind as wild habitat," I often glanced up, in passing, to regard that phrase. It is Sarah's gift, in the words of Gary Snyder, to be crafty and to get the work done. From the OED I quote, "Apprentice: A learner of a craft." Go slow, take care, and mix it up.

"FOOD WITH A PLACE, A FACE, AND A TASTE"

At rest, for the moment, at my desk, I hear the sound of a woodpecker's beak, but the chosen instrument is not beech or hickory:

> Paper wasps' nest reports
> Like great-grandfather cedar
> With woodpecker's: Winter! Winter!
>
> Grass sandles under the hill
> Fill with a swarm of starlings.

I am asked quite often, "What do you do over the winter?" I appreciate the question, though I am usually at a loss for words, for conservation and farming are a continuous occupation, and not easily summarized. I can at least define the dates of the winter season—we harvested the last of the cabbage on December 20, and the first greenhouse seeding date for the next season is scheduled for February 27. Between those dates there is the budget process, the recruiting of apprentices, seed and supply orders, walks, meetings with colleagues, time to listen for winter music—the clack of beech branch against branch, the cardinal's slide through a tangle of vines, the insistence of the Atlantic!

Two weeks ago, at New York's Northeast Organic Farming Association annual winter conference, I was part of a panel focused on how to make the best of a "worst" season. The worst, in the context of difficult seasons, at least in the Northeast, is generally the season defined by rain and rain and more rain. I chose to speak of practical ways to adapt—continue to plant greens (which can flourish in an excess of water), quick!, cultivate when you can in that one afternoon of sun. Start another round of tomatoes in an alternate field, and leave the beans to flower and fruit again and again. At the end of our last season, to my surprise, many of our farm members actually approached me to say, "What a fine season this was!" To be honest, we were improvising—but, to find one form of explanation, please recall the enchantment of a prayer stick planted in a field of rye.

The organic farming movement is at a critical juncture, and from the tip of this fertile island we are listening to the national discussion. In 1990, under the direction of Senator Patrick Leahy, chairman of the Senate agriculture committee, the first Organic Foods Production Act (OFPA) was introduced, which called for the establishment of national organic standards. Before that time a number of organizations, scattered across the country, had created independent sets of standard practices, researched and compiled through an organized grassroots network of dedicated farmers and food activists. In 1979, the California Certified Organic Farmers association (CCOF) helped to create the first state program. In December of 1997, the U.S. Department of Agriculture published the original proposal for national organic standards, under the jurisdiction of the NOP, the National Organic Program. The USDA received a massive outpouring of comments, over 275,000, and 99 percent of the commentary was opposed to the standards as issued. The glaring problem was that the first proposal sanctioned the use of sewage sludge, bioengineered seeds, and irradiation in organic systems. One week following the deadline for commentary, with unprecedented speed, the USDA withdrew the original proposal for further consideration. The new national standards were issued early in 2001, with the exclusion of "the big three," and, after further discussion, the national ruling officially came into effect in October of 2002. Now, in order to use the word "organic," a farmer—and this applies to processors and handlers as well—must be certified by an organization that is accredited by the USDA. Any organization actively certifying prior to the existence of the national ruling had to apply to be accredited, to the USDA, in order to continue to do business. That process, for small organizations, and I speak from experience, was costly in more ways than one.

When the Organic Foods Production Act was originally passed, the organic community successfully lobbied for a National Organic Standards Board (NOSB), which would hopefully balance the authority held by the USDA. The overall intention was to create a partnership between the varied and growing organic community and the USDA, not a simple task. Meanwhile, the organic industry (there is a stress in terminology here) continues to grow at a rate of over 20 percent per year, which has attracted considerable attention. According to the Organic Trade Association (OTA), the United States market is projected to reach a value of $30.7 billion by 2007; at the present rate of increase it is projected that organic food will claim 10 percent of the market share by 2010.

When the National Organic Program went into effect, just a few years ago, there were about forty independent or state-operated organic certifiers throughout the United States. At the time of this writing that number has increased to over 125. Why this sudden interest, especially on the regulatory horizon, in what for years was assumed to be a fringe occupation? How concerned should a small farmer, or a community, be with the details of certification or regulation? Now that food produced by sustainable methods is reaching more people, how do we interest more farmers and educators in the cause? I could continue to pose questions, but I will instead turn it over to Michael Sligh, who offers this paragraph in an article included in *Fatal Harvest*, "Organics at the Crossroads":

The new national rule remains controversial, and how it is implemented will determine its impact on organic integrity. Some very basic questions still remain: Will the rule help the early farmer-innovators of organic agriculture or hurt them? Will the costs, red tape, and paperwork drive the small scale farmer out of organic? Will the rule allow the entry of industrial style confinement livestock operations? Will its regulations enhance or hurt consumer confidence? We must fight for answers to these questions that will ensure fairness and integrity, that will ensure the marriage of values and standards. This is an ongoing struggle for food with a place, a face, and a taste.

The debate continues to heat up, as I am writing. When the NOP issued a number of "directives," which were objectionable to many in the organic community; even the NOSB, meant to advise the NOP, prepared a letter of protest. By issuing directives, without soliciting public comment, the NOP subverted the regulatory process, thus alienating many of those who helped to found the program. In one of the first tests of the new regulations, a Massachusetts certifier, after denying certification to a chicken farmer—who offered his birds no access to the outside, a clear violation of the rule—was itself overruled by the USDA. Is it possible for the person on the street, or in the field, not to be confused?

Elizabeth Henderson, who has monitored this process on a national level since the beginning, comments,

> . . . using organic techniques does not mean simply substituting organic inputs for a conventional one. The most basic organic technique is to observe your farm: what are the complex interrelationships among crops, soils, wildlife. As organic farmers we take this circle wider—we observe the relationships between our farms

and the surrounding community, between our region and the rest of the earth. . . . Organic agriculture is not just a method of production—it is an attitude and an approach towards the world. Organic farming has developed in this country without the benefit of university support, government subsidies, or corporate influence. . . .

Disturbed by the recent directives, and by the apparent confusion associated with the implementation of the national regulations, the National Committee for Sustainable Agriculture is creating a National Organic Action Plan, to advocate for significant changes to the national program, perhaps to include a revision of the original "production act."

When I consider the kinds of complications that have followed after the establishment of the National Organic Program, I tend to side with Charles Waters, who has published *Acres USA* for over thirty years:

> Well, first of all, the term organic has been legislated. For almost 30 years, I wrote editorials begging the organic producers, Don't go to your state and your federal government asking for regulations. . . . What do we do to protect the gains we've made? Just keep right on doing what we're doing. Sell direct to the consumer. Develop consumer-sustainable agriculture. Keep moving ahead and getting the word out, because more and more people are becoming conscious of the fact that it's cheaper to pay a little bit more for food and a little bit less to the pharmaceutical companies.

Our community farm was founded by a group of families in search of a local source for organic vegetables, so we are sensitive to this national discussion. Now that elements of organic practices are actually discussed on syndicated news programs, and included on the editorial page of the *New York Times*, there is a change in the questions posed by our farm members. One member, visibly agitated, rushed to ask me, "We don't spread manure on our fields right before planting seeds, do we?"

I patiently described the difference between compost—which revitalizes our soils made anemic by another style of farming—and manure, but I am basically disturbed by this line of questioning. Those who chose to become members of a CSA farm are certainly among the most curious and educated of consumers (citizens), yet I am surprised by the significant gaps in knowledge most eaters have concerning their food and food sources. Community farming, and community gardens, can inspire trust in a farmer or in a piece of land, and this is a significant action.

How do I explain to listening farm members the fact that, under the existing NOP regulations, I now have to list our compost applications as manure spreading? This is because I am unable and unwilling to turn our compost piles a total of five times within a fifteen-day period, and prove that the pile hovered within a temperature range of 131 to 170 degrees Fahrenheit for that period. There have been many objections to this part of the national rule, and the USDA even appointed a panel of compost experts to deliver a recommendation concerning the letter of the law. At the time of this writing, the recommendations—which support responsible and tested practices—have been ignored. But I am allowed to spread fresh manure on the fields—which I have never done—as long as the application precedes the harvest of a crop by ninety days. The rule requires that I designate our compost—aged and turned over a period ranging from one and a half to two years—as not what it is.

For over ten years, in order to control the Colorado potato beetle, as I described in another chapter, we have used BT, *Bacillus thuringiensis*, bacteria found in the soil. Under the USDA ruling, this biological insecticide is no longer allowed, because of an inert ingredient that, so far, I have been unable to track down. Instead, I can make my choice from a number of "broad spectrum" insecticides, natural substances now listed as organically approved. BT is specific, it targets the potato beetles; a broad spectrum, once sprayed, affects everybody.

So I followed the rules this year, adjusted my practices, studied the sources and recommendations, and chose a likely solution for the pesky beetle. It didn't work. I doubled the application rate, and it still didn't work. By that time the beetles had devoured entire rows of plants, but, because the crop was potatoes, I was unwilling to surrender. I found a source for a new product, Entrust, at the time unlisted in my catalogues, made by the Dow Corporation, part of the approved list for organic farmers. It worked; it killed everything in its path, and saved a portion of the potato crop. I adhered to the rules, submitted my "Spray Record" for certification purposes (which I had honored for ten years prior to the NOP regulations), and lost several thousand dollars.

How concerned should a farmer, or a community, be about the details of certification or regulation? Very.

In March, Paul H. and I seeded clover on twenty-five acres of Amagansett loam, by hand. The first day we stayed ahead of the tractor, which raked in the seed we sowed, and by day's end we had walked, spinning seed, some nineteen miles. That clover, roots reaching down four or five feet to draw up nutrients, created a carpet, live green matter, tempered to accept water. Given the labor nature expends to make one inch of topsoil, it is the least we can do to prevent erosion and aid in the formation of humus. It is the charm of clover, if well seeded and repeatedly mowed, to stimulate life in the soil and to lay down increased organic matter. Now, in winter, accustomed to the cold, the clover is thick and vibrant. For years we have worked with clovers and the whole of the biotic community to build a healthy soil in this fine island place. Silt loam, given care, will help to create an ecological balance, and also provide nests of grass under the hill, for passing starlings.

IN THE CIRCLE AT THE CENTER

All winter long in Cornwall, Edgar would pass by our cottage on Love Lane, to and from the cliff meadows where he cut violets, the winter flower. He laid them carefully in a basket and searched the stone hedgerows for the near-perfect ivy leaves to be used for backing for each bunch. Darkness would descend before 4:00 PM, and the lane was generally punctuated with puddles and muck. Edgar would still call out to me at dusk, although our conversations were shortened at this time of year. We huddled under the hedge pretending to shelter from the drizzle and discussed the weather, the price of violets, the seed potatoes already sprouting in boxes. With no warning he would wheel about, turn on his heel, shout "I'm off!" and disappear into the shadows of Love Lane.

Once at dusk, on a rare dry day he boasted to Megan and me of his immunity to that amazing plant, stinging nettles. Nettles are everywhere in the landscape of Penwith—along the edges of every path, hiding under ornamentals in the garden, leaping out of the stone walls. When we looked at him with some suspicion he dove into a nearby hedge, emerged with handfuls of potent-looking greenery, and proceeded to wash his hands with the pointed leaves and stems of nettles. When he offered me the stinging soap I graciously declined; though I am of Celtic lineage and also a believer in nettle soup, I've researched it (!) and I have zero immunity to the stuff.

Having apparently proven his point and added his standard parting shout (with exaggerated gusto), he scurried off down the lane. Megan and I lingered, squinting into the shadows. Toward the end of the lane, before he turned to descend the stone steps to the village, he paused, dropped his arms to his sides, and yes, shook his stinging hands. (We kept the secret to ourselves.)

The Cornish winter is dark and damp and it can be astonishingly rough, but it is soon over. Often by late January the shoots of daffodils and narcissi emerge, and the bell-shaped blossoms can follow in mid-February. Edgar and his wife, Dora, spent many winter evenings counting and banding violets—twenty flowers to a bunch, backed by precisely three ivy leaves—and packing tiny bouquets into shoe boxes destined for Covent Garden. When the days began to lengthen and some scent of spring came by on the breeze, Edgar would add some song to accompany a greeting or a good-bye. "Away . . . I'm bound away . . ." is the melodic phrase I repeat to the migrating birds on this other peninsula. And I visualize the man from Mousehole who would part the fuchsia hedge with rough hands, spout some seed wisdom, and finish with a verse of "I'll take you home again, Kathleen."

Encased in ice for a few days, kale and collard greens thaw today and shake off crystals, and are sweeter than ever. A gardener tries to learn from plants such secrets as describe the fluidity of the invisible. We can name the action that moves water through the capillaries of stems, but do we know how to name that which creates resiliency in a living organism, the individual essence of a plant? The lifeblood of these greens is part of the choir of winter that shakes last leaves and nuts from the beech and pushes buds to appear on apple shoots. The poet-doctor from New Jersey, William Carlos Williams, articulated this central theme: "No ideas but in things. . . ." Walking in the winter orchard or field I face things directly (not ideas), eye to eye with bare branch, cold curled greenery, or the bright cardinal in flight against the gray oaks.

Tiny red stars suspended in a cool green, the berries of American holly shutter in the wind among the rust colors of beech, hickory, and bittersweet. Barred Rocks, Wyandottes, and Speckled Sussex huddle together on apple-wood roosts. Open the greenhouse door and you will witness an out-of-season green—arugula, mizuna, and red mustard producing vibrant, crisp leaves sheltered within the hoophouse.

Walking out from among the hollies I am greeted by two hawks. They fall from the tall hickory and glide without a wing beat over the brown grasses of the valley. In the quiet of this season and seasoned by mist the speech of sparrows and chickadees is casual. The tips of apple branches are a deep red against the cool blue of sky. These apple buds ripen so slowly the process is invisible—in the words of Elizabeth Bishop, "For Time is / nothing if not amenable."

After the winter solstice the days quietly grow longer. Unable to harvest the full crop of late carrots, we covered what remained in the soil with a very thick straw mulch. Snow is falling on the stems of the rye straw we cut from the field in June. Snow is falling down through the rough grain we've scattered over the sweet roots left in the soil. Snow is melting into waterdrops that wet the tops of roots, the winter harvest. Over the hedgerow that slows the winter wind snow settles on the stems of wild bramble. As flakes are falling the hedge comes to resemble a fluid river, with whitecaps tossing above the field. Snow is falling on clover used to cover the field; small leaves now appear as individual diamonds before the blanket of whiteness descends. Snow falls on the sassafras trees, the lone birch, the oaks, the beech and hickory. Snow rises on a drift of wind to brush the bare olives. Whiteness collects on oats and rye and bellbeans, on field peas and vetch, and on seeds sleeping in the earth. Snow is falling on the leaves of herbs scattered in the circle at the center of the farm—fennel, sage, lemon balm, oregano, thyme, savory, tarragon, and mint. Here on winter ground I learn to trust in "the faintly visible traces of the world."

"THE SPIRIT UNSEEN"

As the days begin to lengthen and the ground to thaw, the seed packets arrive, and again we have a clutter on the worktable. Though I am not new to the process, each year I sense the urgency of spring, and renewal, with the arrival of a myriad of seeds. The names alone can be magical, suggestive of intriguing places and unknown lineage—Nero di Toscana, Blacktail Mountain, Cosmonaut Volkov, Rouge Vif d'Etampes, Queensland Blue, Jaune Flammée, Cherokee Purple, and Paul Robeson. It may be that we plant over two hundred varieties yearly just to taste the names. Anyone who has named a child will recognize the inherent mystery in the act of naming, part of the mystery of language itself. I begin to know a plant through the resonance of a name, and the name unfolds into cotyledons, foliage, and the carriage of stem and branch. Susan Brind Morrow writes,

> Words begin as description. They are prismatic, vehicles of hidden, deeper shades of thought. You can hold them up at different angles until the light bursts through in an unexpected color. The word carries the living thing concealed across millennia.

One of our principal suppliers, Fedco, a Maine seed cooperative, posed this question in their catalogue (penned by the founder, C. R. Lawn): "Do you know where your seed comes from?" The answer immediately follows: "Probably not, unless you save your own." The simple answer, no, would be spoken again, by most people, in response to a similar question: "Do you know where your food comes from?"

Very few farmers, at least in this country, save a substantial portion of their own seed, though this would come as a surprise to the public—many people may never have entertained the question. There is a movement now, encouraged by various seed savers associations—such as the Seed Savers Exchange, the Scatterseed Project, Native Seeds/SEARCH—and by the Public Seed Initiative, to retrain farmers and gardeners in the art of seed production, harvesting, and storage. This ancient practice has not been ignored, but economic realities have forced most farmers to concentrate on growing crops and marketing, and to leave the art of seed saving and distribution to others. And more specifically, institutional and market forces are equally responsible for what has been termed a "significant lag in organic seed and breeding efforts."

Throughout the nineteenth century, and before, of course, farmers and gardeners had commonly saved seeds and also experimented with seed selection and backyard breeding. In the 1930s, with the introduction of the hybridization process, beginning with sweet corn, the business of saving seed began to change. Craig Holdrege defines a hybrid like this: "In narrow terms, the progeny of a cross between two varieties or races of the same species, which themselves have been produced by repeated self-fertilization or inbreeding. More generally, the progeny of a cross between parents of different genetic types or different species."

Hybridization allowed seed breeders to choose for desirable characteristics, among diverse varieties. This style of breeding can result in something called heterosis, or hybrid vigor, which can give the grower a plant with either increased sweetness, or disease resistance, or early ripening—for one year only. Those last three words should be underlined, so that the reader understands that the seed of plants created through the process of hybridization will not

breed true. As C. R. Lawn reports, "Humans have been experiment-
ing with plant breeding for thousands of years. Hybridization took
human intervention a giant step further." We will have to attend to
the ethical choices offered, and those choices offered by the introduction of genetically engineered seed, in the next book.

By the end of the twentieth century, within the framework of
our industrial system, the control of seeds had been concentrated in
the hands of a few multinationals. Companies like Fedco, in an attempt to support a more sustainable agricultural system, look for
seed in many places: "Like all other retail seed companies, we
mostly purchase quality seed grown in optimum climatic conditions by expert seedpeople in Idaho, Washington, Oregon, California, and Colorado, or imported from Japan, France, Holland,
Denmark, Germany, Switzerland or Italy." There are many reasons
to appreciate the people at Fedco, which still operates as a co-op; we
include on that list their dedication to sustainable farming practices
and to cooperation among farmers, their educational mission, their
quirky sense of humor, and their imaginative seed varietal descrip-
tions. We are also understanding when they are difficult to reach after April 15. Their seed sales division is closed until the following
winter; C. R. Lawn and Nikos and the crew are out in the field testing the varieties that they offer in the cool climate of Maine.

Increasingly, a number of seed suppliers are beginning to create
their own trials programs, and to research "on farm" sources for traditional open pollinated varieties. Our seed supply in this country is
presently being reinvigorated through a grassroots network of individual gardeners, farmers, enlightened extension agents, and savvy
seed companies.

There are about two billion small farmers in the rest of the
world quietly saving seed, and therefore protecting biodiversity,
even while corporate hegemony threatens their survival. The spread
of seed stock that contains GMOs (genetically modified organisms),
by the multinationals, is a cause of great concern throughout Eu-

rope, Africa, and Asia, though, in general, the public in this country remains very sleepy on this issue.

All of the seed companies that we place orders with subscribe to the "Safe Seed Pledge," which reads like this:

> Agriculture and seeds provide the basis upon which our lives depend. We must protect this foundation as a safe and genetically stable source for future generations. For the benefit of all farmers, gardeners, and consumers who want an alternative, we pledge that we do not knowingly buy or sell genetically engineered seeds or plants. The mechanical transfer of genetic material outside of natural methods and between genera, families, or kingdoms poses great biological risks as well as economic, political, and cultural threats. We feel that genetically engineered varieties have been insufficiently tested prior to public release. More research and testing is necessary to further assess the potential risks to genetically engineered seeds. Further, we wish to support agricultural progress that leads to healthier soils, genetically diverse agricultural ecosystems, and ultimately healthy people and communities.

I know, through conversations with Quail Hill Farm members, that most consumers assume that organic farmers purchase and plant organic seed. Until the arrival of the USDA National Organic Program (NOP) this was far from true. An adequate supply of organically produced seed stock simply did not, and still does not, exist. The NOP rules now state that, in order to be certified organic, a farmer must use organically grown seed unless none is available for a specific variety. This can lead to hardship for small farmers, who must now carry out a cross search for each variety, and who are required by law to pay a premium of two to three times (or more) for certified organic seed, regardless of their past record as a committed steward of land. There is a great opportunity here—to expand the production and availability of organic seed stock—but what if the timing for such a strict requirement forces more farmers out of business? Wouldn't it be wiser for a federal program to research and ensure seed availability before creating regulations, as was done in Europe, where a similar program was brought in gradually? What if the USDA doubled the share of research dollars allocated to organic agriculture (to 2 percent!) in order to stimulate seed saving initiatives, and in support of biodiversity? We should be hopeful, in any case, that increased demand will lead to increased organic seed production, and an expansion in acreage farmed through the use of ecological or organic practices.

High Mowing Seeds, of Wolcott, Vermont, this year included with the seed shipment a "Seed Saving Guide for Gardeners and Farmers." I still retain a copy of their first catalogue—a one-page mimeographed sheet, mailed out by founder Tom Stearns at the ripe age of twenty. Tom notes that he founded High Mowing in 1995 "out of a concern for the loss of genetic diversity among cultivated plants." All of the seeds he lists are certified organic, which means that business is on the rise following the implementation of the NOP, in October 2002. As a preface to his seed saving guide, Tom notes, "I learned what I could from several sources but a simple guide like this would have been a great help to get me started. I hope it is to you."

It is obvious that Tom has something other in mind than to generate future business for High Mowing Seeds. Listen to the clear, simple seed saving instructions for spinach:

> Wind pollinated. Spinach varieties must be isolated by ¼ mile to prevent cross pollination by wind. Physical barriers such as tree lines, buildings or woods may make it possible to use a shorter distance. Allow plants to bolt and set seed. Some staking may be necessary as plants

may reach 3' in height. When seeds are dry, harvest the entire plant and thresh on a tarp. A ½" screen on top of a ¼" and ⅛" is helpful for cleaning. Spinach seed remains viable for 3–5 years under cool and dry storage conditions.

Many other seed companies, such as Fedco, Southern Exposure Seed Exchange, and Abundant Life, also give instruction to their customers to encourage seed saving and biodiversity.

I confess that I am not ready when the seed catalogues start to arrive around Thanksgiving (earlier every year). I close my eyes, and they are stacked in a carton until after the new year. I am hesitant to invest in a new year before carrots, turnips, rutabaga, and broccoli are secure in the root cellar. But what a delight when the time comes. Leafing through the pages I am willing to take some chances; I am engaged foremost by the process of discovery, and fully aware of the labor of others to provide such a choice in seeds. In Johnny's of Maine I find Yukina, a savoyed leaf version of a perennial favorite, tatsoi. After repeated failures with the varietal Golden Beet, I discover Yellow Cylindrical Beet in Baker Creek Heirloom Seeds, a mangel that is sweet when harvested young, and thinning is not required. Fedco carries Chioggia, a candy-striped, swirled beet that most people mistake for a turnip or radish. Seed Savers Exchange offers a beautiful tomato known as Roman Candle, sweet tasting with few seeds, and the yellow stripes dazzle like flame on the red skin. From late January until mid-March I return to the catalogues, until it is time to shift to field work. By the end of the process our seed stocks count over 225 varieties, an adequate number to entice our CSA harvesters to the farm.

Edward O. Wilson comments, "Great truths are sometimes so enveloping and exist in such plain view as to be invisible. One of them is the dominance on the land of flowering plants and insects."

Three billion years ago, life as we know it began to develop in the oceans. For aeons, until the conifers arrived, roughly 290 million years ago, the ancient plants developed within and depended upon water for reproduction. The conifers developed pollen grains to enclose sperms, which could take flight on the wind to reach eggs in other cones. This was the beginning of seeds—an egg fertilized by pollen, and protected by a waterproof coat. Seeds are really infantile plants that are fed and protected until they can survive on their own. The gymnosperms—pines, larches, spruce, fir, yew, cypress, and cedar—are "naked seeded" plants, because their seed is not completely enclosed in a husk or fruit. Donald Culross Peattie writes, "But the seed is weighted with a great thing. Within even the tiniest lies the germ of a fetal plantlet, its fat cotyledons and first baby leaves still crumpled in darkness, its primary rootlet ready to thrust and suckle at the breast of the earth." As a testament to the success of the first seed plants, one third of the forests throughout the globe consist of conifers.

Wind as a vehicle for pollen, the most ancient method of dispersal, is relatively efficient, but Mother Nature had in mind a more sophisticated system. So, when the first flowering plants appeared, 120 million years ago, they proved to be so adaptable and versatile that they have come to define the vegetative kingdom on earth. The flowering world—populated by the angiosperms—is made up of over two hundred thousand species.

Conceived in like architecture, I find it impossible to imagine a world without seeds. Earth and seeds go together, though in cosmological terms, the wedding was only recently performed. Each seed shelters in a flower until it is time for it to travel. This is part of the miracle—seeds can choose the vehicle. A blackbird's beak, the steel shank of a harrow, the garden trowel, or oat straw forked over in spring. For those intent on saving seeds, the trick is to be there to catch them at the right moment.

The environmental activist Vandana Shiva, in an exquisite and sobering book, *Stolen Harvest*, writes: "The seed, for the farmer, is not merely the source of future plants and food; it is the storage place of culture and history. Seed is the first link in the food chain. Seed is the ultimate symbol of food security."

We begin to seed in trays destined for the 72-degree greenhouse in late February, early March. The alliums, sensitive to light and day-light hours, are the first to be planted, accompanied by some herbs. Each onion seed, each seed of leek or parsley, is placed by hand in a cell of a tray that has been packed with our homemade seed-starter mix. Given the volume we hope to produce, we welcome the eighth-grade class that can complete the seeding of forty trays in less than an hour (128 cells $\times$ 3 onion seeds per cell $\times$ 40 trays = 15,360 potential onions). For the sake of morale I praise the speed of the students, but secretly what pleases me is the contact between hand and seed. The infant plant is invisible, secure in a child's palm, but the contact between the physical and potential is visible. It is at the moment when I pick up the wand to water the allium seeds, af-ter the class with my daughter, Rowenna, has left, that I recall a brief story from the Chandogya Upanishad:

> When Svetaketu, at his father's bidding, had brought
> a ripe fruit from the banyan tree, his father said to him,
> "Split the fruit in two, dear son."
> "Here you are. I have split it in two."
> "What do you find there?"
> "Innumerable tiny seeds."
> "Then take one of the seeds and split it."
> "I have split the seed."
> "And what do you find there?"
> "Why, nothing, nothing at all."
> "Ah, dear son, but this great tree cannot possibly come from nothing. Even if you cannot see with your eyes that subtle something in the seed which produces

this mighty form, it is present nonetheless. That is the power, that is the spirit unseen, which pervades everywhere and is all things. Have faith! That is the spirit which lies at the root of all existence, and that also art thou, O Svetaketu."

SPRING

. . . but spring
is everlasting
resurrection.

—BASIL BUNTING,
FIRST BOOK OF ODES: I, 1924

ONE AMONG MANY

After two days of sun and a strong wind following a weekend of heavy spring rains, the soil is sufficiently dried out to take the weight of a man and tractor. And it is time to transplant the first lettuce onto Hurricane Hill, to mature into lush heads, we hope, for the first harvest day. The seedling trays sparkle with a variety of brown, red, and green—leaf lettuce, butterhead, and romaine, with names such as Red Ice, Ermosa, Sierra, Italianischer, Forellenschluss (speckled like a trout). Before we place them in the soil, we prepare a bath of well water and fish emulsion, and then immerse the full trays—a practice that always leads to exclamations from the new apprentices. Our theory—give the roots of baby plants a good drink to ease the shock of transplanting.

For the next weeks, throughout the month of May, we watch closely for the planting windows, to take advantage of the spring rains. Trays and trays of young plants, seeded in late February and early March, cry out to go into the ground—they have exhausted the nutrients in the well-structured cells of our transplant trays. Lettuce is followed by parsley in the field, onions, scallions, the first hearty flowers, and Red Russian, Lacinato, and Winterbor—three varieties of kale that will stand in the field into January. At the same time, and on a two- to three-week rotation, we are direct-seeding early greens, radish, turnips, carrots, and beets. In a place surrounded by cool ocean water, and daily washed by an ocean breeze, it is impossible to expect instant gratification. In the middle of May, with the exception of a few hot days, we are still wearing clothes three layers thick as we drop plant after plant into the loam. I have learned to wait until the soil warms, and the moon is on the rise, to give the first seeds the best chance to awaken.

The process of seeding into trays is accompanied by the dilemma of where to put them. Once our three greenhouses are full we shift the most mature plants to a cold frame—they are exposed during the day and covered at night—to harden them off. In the final stage before being planted into the ground all transplants are introduced to full days in the open air. If the ground is too wet or cold for planting, the question is—where to hold them for the time being? At some stage in May we daily determine which tomatoes to move from the heated to the unheated greenhouse, which herbs to shift to the cold frame, where to germinate the third seeding of lettuce—if we should forget to seed celeriac, will we be forgiven by the rare individual who knows what it is?

Last autumn, with the help of some robust AmeriCorps volunteers, we carefully and meticulously weeded the asparagus patch. The Greeks named this plant "asparagos," meaning "to swell," because of the production of early shoots. As hard as we work to avoid it from happening, this member of the lily family tends to attract grass and weeds. It is one thing to cultivate and maintain croppings of annual plants, but it is quite another to care for the perennials. Asparagus is a special challenge, for just when the time for harvesting spears draws to a close there are a thousand tasks to tend to elsewhere. Weed seeds and the runners of quack grass are listening, and ready, for just such an opportunity. After our first asparagus patch—planted in our premier season—was overcome seven years later, we did not consider surrender. The strong, sweet taste of early spears of Purple Passion was sufficient to suggest replanting.

Asparagus is native to both Europe and Asia, where it loves to grow in the wild by the edge of the sea. For thousands of years *Asparagus officinalis* was primarily a medicinal plant, supplying vitamin A, vitamin C, and iron to those who had survived the winter on roots. It is said that a certain king of France chose as his personal gardener the fellow who could provide him with asparagus throughout the year (how did he do it?).

So now we are six years into our second attempt, and I have heard of asparagus beds producing a fine crop thirty years later. The trick is to keep the patch clean—to give the crowns ample chance to send up stronger and fuller spears.

I love the process of planting asparagus—the job is simple and satisfying, and the plant has the look and character of a cultivar with a hearty ancestry. First one digs a trench, roughly ten inches deep. Then the crowns are laid in the trench, with spaghetti-like roots directed east and west of the crown, to just touch the roots of the next crown. A small amount of soil is raked over the plants to cover them, but not to fill the trench. When the crowns send up the first spears, two weeks later, it is time to cover them again, and so on, until the trench is gradually filled. The true patience of a gardener is now put to a test—one must wait a year, until the plants are more secure and nourished, to taste the stalks.

Each successive spring, if fed with good compost and, in most locations, some lime, asparagus spears will be among the first food of the year, and the taste, fresh from the field, according to our farm members, is unequaled. The harvest season is brief, and to end it— a willful act—again requires a reserve of patience from the gardener or farmer. At the end of June, if one desires a crop the following year, the harvest is over; asparagus lovers must cast their eyes elsewhere, and urge their hands to harvest scallions, fennel, or cilantro instead. The crowns must be given freedom to direct roots deep into the soil, to draw up nutrients that will nourish the plant for another year. The powerful roots of asparagus reach down five to six feet, in search of what is needed to produce strong spears. Aboveground the shoots radiate out into graceful ferns; the stalks harden and stand throughout winter. The beauty of the plant—first as edible spears, then as an ornamental—survives the seasons.

It was our intention, in the autumn, after hand cultivation, to mulch the asparagus patch with oat straw, and then to harvest and enjoy the spears of early spring. But somehow some rye straw, with hearty seeds, found its way into our mulch. The result—this spring we are weeding out the regrowth of rye, just as the first asparagus shoots rise from the straw. Asparagus, self-confident and delicious, continues to demand attention. And we continue to accept the invitation.

In the grass that swallowed our original asparagus patch, tender spears continue to push through, fifteen years after the crowns were laid into the trench. A few farm members remember the patch, and each spring they comb the grass, thankful for this plant's persistence. The rock that celebrates Deborah Light's gift of land is there, not far from the spreading limbs of a pin oak tree we planted in 1990. When the idea for a plaque was suggested, I searched the woodlands surrounding Quail Hill for the rock that would sing. I found it on a neighbor's land—six hundred pounds of granite—and he agreed to surrender the rock to honor Deborah. We moved it half a mile to where it now rests, by some miracle of tractor and trailer, and will. I remember having a certain lack of confidence in the procedure, and also my thought: "Will she like the rock?"

She does. The inscription reads:

DEBORAH ANN LIGHT PRESERVE
192 acres
Donated to the Peconic Land Trust
January 25, 1995

In recognition of her love of the land
And her generosity to the community.

With the rock in place, secure on a new pillow of silt loam, Deborah is still engaged with this place. Speaking from near Main Street, Sag Harbor, her new home, she told me, "At one time, out for a walk, if I would climb Quail Hill and crouch down, and, if I

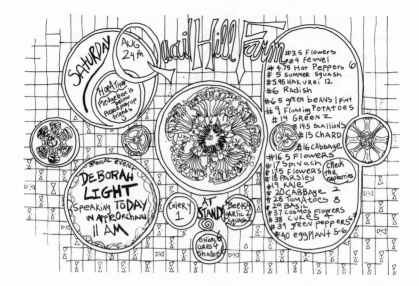

really squinted with my eyes and looked out, I owned all the land that I could see."

. Today I happened to read in a book by the poet Lorine Niedecker some words that have relevance:

> Black Hawk held: In reason
> Land cannot be sold,
> Only things to be carried away. . . .

Deborah gave her land away because she did not consider it solely "hers." Land is not, as we have come to value it, only a bundle of rights; it is, as Chuck Matthei, and before him, Native American elders, pointed out, a complex web of relationships. Deborah is linked to the land within that web, and we are entwined with the filament.

I remember her almost daily, as I work with the land, because her gift is everywhere revealed—in the circus of blossoms that covers the hill, the stand of cedars in the center of the valley, in the heartwood of the beech trees. The granite stone bearing the words honors her, as do the people who come to harvest from the land. She is, I believe, inextricably linked to the whole web of relationships that indigenous humans have honored for millennia. Common to this ground, one among many:

> I speak from the hill near to the sea:
>
> I am the wind that moves the grass.
> I am the iron within the stone.
> I am the water that seeks the valley.
> I am the bark of oak, heartwood of holly.
> I am the seed within the pod,
>> within the tear,
>>> within the tide.
> I am the sky woman,
>> invisible within the wing
> that touches ground and air
>> to rise and sing. . . .*

---

*Suggested by the "Alphabet Calendar" of Amergin, the bard of the Milesians, sometimes considered to be the first poet of Ireland.

A LETTER

A few years ago, on a busy Saturday harvest day, as I was thinning the cucumber patch, a loyal farm member called out to me, through the steel and nylon line of the deer fence: "Have you written another book yet?"

When I published a special edition of poetry, accompanied by woodcuts, crafted and printed in England by the Cornish-Irish artist Breon O'Casey, she bought a copy, and now she was hoping for another. "You are the answer to a writer's prayer," I replied, "but, I am sorry to say, I haven't found the time."

Two minutes later, or maybe it was three, another veteran member of the community farm actually leaned in through the deer fence to say: "You know, I've always admired your letters, and I wonder, have you ever thought of putting it all together into a book? I'm an editor, and I would love to help make it happen."

After a fruitful conversation with Paul B., I went back to check our "Stella Natura," the biodynamic calendar we use for planting dates, just to see which of the stars or planets were aligned in my favor on that particular day. I discovered it was a good day to harvest fruit.

I consider it "sufficient unto the day" to close this book with that which began it, many years ago, in response to a community of people with an idea and a practical purpose—to find a ready source for fresh, local food. I am willing to make a wild guess that the impulse was also generated through the soil, not only by those walking upon it. This community is still in agreement with the thought expressed by William McDonough: "I'm interested in fecundity, and celebrations of nature's abundance and designs that enrich life."

February 26, 2004

Dear Farm Members:

After twenty-four hours of rain, a few weeks ago, with the ground still frozen, two lakes appeared here at Quail Hill. We have had ponds before—in the valley, by the raspberries, and on Hurricane Hill, surrounding the wild vines and asters. But this winter, the coldest in 110 years I have heard, is perfectly suited to small lake formation. For days the old apple trees and the young raspberries were encased in ice, until a brief thaw arrived and the winter soil accepted the excess of water. Some days of brilliant sun have loosened the top inch of soil, but under, the ground still believes in winter. When I stir the leaves under the beech and oaks I find the reassuring evidence of earthworms rising to travel on the soil surface. Give us some time and we will be traveling there too, to sow some seeds.

Welcome to our fifteenth year of organic growing in north Amagansett, at Quail Hill Farm. We started with a small group of families in search of a reliable source of fresh organic vegetables, and a land trust with a mission to conserve land and community. Now we have grown to about two hundred families who take part in either a summer or winter share, a place open to members, lots of kids, flocks of starlings, a couple of red-tailed hawks, lacewings, honeybees, tree swallows, and hoptoads. In late January I was part of a team of four, at the annual New York Northeast Organic Farming Association conference, to present a full-day CSA training session. I learned then that Quail Hill Farm (founded in 1988 and renamed twice), along with Buttermilk CSA , shares the claim to be the oldest CSA in New York State. So, are we older and wiser? I, myself, like to recall a sympathetic sentence directed to me (quietly) by a farm member: "We are still learning leaf . . ."

We are hoping to include 195 shares for the summer season, so please pass the word on to friends of conservation and sustainable agriculture. It is likely, depending on the weather, that the harvest days will begin as June begins, and continue into November. The winter share begins at Thanksgiving, and continues through February. When I conclude this letter I will help prepare the boxes for the final harvest of the 2003–2004 season—we still have supplies of carrots, spuds, cabbage, rutabaga, parsnips, onions, and garlic, all stored here in the Quail Hill shop and root cellar. Next week we begin to set seeds in trays, and very soon the greenhouses will be warm and full of the new energy of seeds sprouting into leaves. You are invited to come and stand and absorb the pleasures of the sprout houses.

The seeds have arrived, and we always delight in unpacking, still a process of discovery. Some of the participants: Bright Lights, Blacktail Mountain, Chioggia, Lutz Green Leaf, Flamingo Feather, Autumn Beauty, Firmament, Fatali, Galeux d'Eysines. We will experiment with some new tomato varieties, of course, and hope to locate them on the morning of the Tomato Tasting. New peppers of color: Buran, Tollies Sweet Italian, and Orange Bell. After an encouraging premier season of sweet potatoes, we'll try it again, and we will also introduce an autumn squash known as Thelma Sanders Sweet Potato. Our traditional potatoes will appear in all shapes, sizes, and colors—we have twenty varieties on order from our supplier, Moose Tubers of Maine.

The ground is warming today, and our hens are laying, as the hours of light increase each day. We began this farm with the intention to improve the health of our soils and to interact with the community, from microbial life within the soil, to bees sipping on the flowers of herbs and apples, to feathered swallows feeding on insects above the cropland. Some recent soil tests confirm the vitality of our work here, though I see it clearly in your faces when you come to harvest Rhubarb chard, Orange thyme, or Autumn Gold berries. Soil fertility reflects the health of a community. Through labor, insight, and conservation season by season we recreate a place for cedars, butterfly weed, sweet basil, and squash, for people, for bob-white and red fox. And for those who carry pollen from golden-rod to their hive home, expert in sensing the natural order. Welcome again to this common ground.

Yours,

AFTERWORD

The land consists of soils, water, plants, and animals, but
health is more than a sufficiency of these comments. It is
a state of vigorous self-renewal in each of them, and in
all collectively.

—ALDO LEOPOLD

Turning ground in the Cornish hillside meadows we would
sometimes stop to gaze out at the sea, one hundred feet below. The small English robin would follow us, to pause on
hilt or handle of a Cornish shovel, looking for fresh food. In that
strongly Christian country Edgar's tenor recital of "Were you there
when they crucified my lord?" harmonized strangely, surely, with
the sound of waves reaching granite, and of jackdaws and black-
backs sweeping through the damp air. He has traveled with me
through this book, and I recall him not simply to eulogize, but to invoke the qualities inherent in a man who lived as a natural-born
steward of land. Edgar passing on the lane with a basket of violets
was more than a symbol of a vanished pastoral. His voice was resonant with the liquid in the air, sap coursing through privet and fuchsia branch, the robin's miniature tenor. Working with a Cornishman
in the cliff meadows of the Penwith peninsula, working here on the
South Fork of another island, I have seen what simple grasses and
wild seeds can give back to the earth. In the locust trees, clovers, and

goldenrod the secret of honey survives. I still listen at Quail Hill to a song carried on the ocean air that fuses with the natural music of each season.

When I began farming here in Amagansett I was told more than once that "Farming is dead on the East End." I cannot readily accept such resignation, though I understand the despair that can lead to it. It is one thing to participate in a campaign to support your local farmers; it is quite another to tackle the institutions that perpetuate the agricultural crisis, which, when considered, can certainly leave us with a sense of hopelessness. In *The Fatal Harvest Reader*, Andrew Kimbrell has selected viewpoints that instead support a new agrarian consciousness that "seeks to heal and restore our relationship with nature, the farmer, and the land."

Wendell Berry observes that "The things that I have tried to defend are less numerous and worse off now than when I started . . ." (forty years ago, he notes). In an afterword to Kimbrell's book, entitled "Hope," Wendell writes:

> What agrarian principles implicitly purpose—and what I explicitly propose in advocating those principles at this time—is a revolt of local small producers and local consumers against the global industrialism of the corporations.

Unless we address the imbalance of power, for the sake of local ecosystems and the life within those systems, we will indeed remain ineffective. I am hesitant to create an adversarial dilemma; but in an era overwhelmed by environmental degradation, I do want to help to create a solution that may encourage the state of harmony between men and land that Aldo Leopold called for.

For years I have presented the model of conservation land trusts to community farm activists, and the model of community farming to land trust advocates, but the marriage of the two in practice remains rare. Three or four years ago an aspiring community gardener, hoping to form a similar partnership, told me that after some research, we were the one working model he could find. I am aware of several new projects throughout the country, but our society is still in the exploratory stages of building a new commons through public/private partnerships and alternative (radical) collaborations that create stability and support real livelihoods. I feel the possibilities for new working relationships are as real and varied as the multiple examples of CSAs and land trusts that have emerged from American soil in the past twenty years.

Our attitudes toward land, and our public policies, are central to the way in which we treat one another, and "others." Chuck Matthei, the founder of Equity Trust, in an address to land conservationists in Burlington, Vermont, spoke of "the challenge of addressing the inextricably linked futures of the people who live on or near [that] land to its survival, and its to theirs." He goes on to say that if we listen to the voices in Congress, in the legislatures, and in town halls,

> . . . one could easily be led to think that public and private interests are fundamentally distinct and inherently antagonistic. But you know and I know from our very practical experience in communities across the country that this is simply not so. We know that property is much more than a set of legal constraints or market calculations, that it is a complex web of relationships, relationships between individuals and their communities, the wildlife, the plant life, and the next generation that will come after all of us. And that that web of relationships links those different parties together in each of the dimensions of property. In the land use area, in the questions of access and governance, and in the distribution of value. . . .

If modern conservation practice is based largely on the notion that property is a bundle of rights, I'd like to suggest that there's a corollary principle which we must embrace and that is that property value is a bundle of values. It comes from many sources. There is no such thing as a property which is absolutely private. There is no property value which derives entirely from the contribution, the investments of labor and capital, by the owner or occupant. The roots of our political dilemma, I believe, lie in our failure to acknowledge the social contributions to value and to treat them prudently, to manage them as a long term investment in the common good. . . .

It's time to recognize the partnership between individuals and community that is inherent in each parcel and lot.

Chuck was articulate and hopeful concerning the social and economic dimensions of conservation: "Property is a formidable institution, but it is not immutable, it is more changeable than most of us realize, and we can change it."

As a steward of the Amagansett fields I love to converse as part of the community of soil, seeds, plants, and animals, but also vital is the conversation we have created as a community of people exploring an ethic. Access to land, when viewed as an abstraction to be defined by "property rights," remains a narrow, restrictive concept. Creative options, and I mean those that encourage a living agricultural system, are born out of a willingness to acknowledge and support the "stability, integrity, and beauty of the biota." At this stage in history we can't really afford to hoard or destroy land. Instead, through readings of wind, wave, and soil we must work to renew the contract between land, sea, and inhabitant.

Tying up the tomatoes, fifteen years ago, I did not anticipate the term of my work here, nor of what that particular communication would lead to. In anticipation of another season, I recently reread the original aims of the *Orion* magazine: "To explore the ethic of humane stewardship; to advance the notion that effective stewardship comes from feelings of respect and admiration for the earth. . . ." The Vermont teacher and writer John Elder comments, "In education and conservation alike, we must pursue stewardship not simply as the maintenance of valuable resources, but also as a way of fostering a broader experience of democracy and community."

John continues, "We also enter the story of a place through the narrative of our individual lives." We enter the story of a place like Quail Hill now through a pattern of lives that meet to form a collective response to soil, flower, and fruit. The narrative is revised and enlarged when a hand reaches to cut some cosmos, when someone kneels to pluck a ripe Rosa Bianca. Another hand whisks away pigweed or lamb's-quarters, a worker's hoe stirs soil at the base of broccoli—this is the cultivation of a sense of place. To cultivate is also to expand the boundaries of home, to enter into conversation with the ground of being, to prepare the seedbed for change.

There is an invisible thread that links time, place, and the being who lives in a particular space. I am aware of it when I sow seeds into Amagansett silt loam; a melody is suggested by the wind, and resembles the invitation of a child. When the sun rises and a thin mist hovers over orchard grass, thrush song falls within the cedars. The star Rigel disappears, Jupiter fades from the sky, a seed germinates in the warming soil, my sons and daughter rise to the day, I cultivate a story of home. And I am reminded of this phrase by Henry Bugbee: "Our true home is wilderness, even the world of every day."

CADENCE

Sparrow at song
In budding willow

And on rust bracken.
This almost earth

Shares his flute
Of green to yellow.

The lyric of place
Inflects like wood—
Surface grain and leaf lace.

ACKNOWLEDGMENTS

It has not proved possible within the scope of this book to report fairly on the broader work carried out by the Peconic Land Trust, my employer. Quail Hill Farm is indeed a project of the trust, and since the original donation of twenty acres of land by Deborah Light, the trust has worked some magic in order to protect more than 650 acres of land in north Amagansett, contiguous with the farm (PLT has protected more than 8,000 acres in total on the eastern end of Long Island). Much of the success of the trust is the result of the founder's vision. John Halsey, with his intelligence, heart, determination, and deep feeling for the land at the fish tail of Long Island, has created not only conserved landscapes, but intangible benefits for people, plants, and wildlife. I thank him for choosing to hire a poet (there can be risks).

I would also like to thank all of my colleagues at PLT, with whom I have shared many years of experimentation, planning, meeting, conversation, and laughter. I would especially like to thank: Pam Greene ("It's just me again!"), Laura Fischer, Rebecca Chapman, Maria Socko, Marsha Kenny, Denise Markut, Graham Hawks, Tim Caufield, Dawn Haight, Steve Rendell, Marie Gallinari, and Donna Bova. A number of PLT board members—past and present—have offered continuous encouragement and support: Tom Williams, Blair McCaslin, Deborah Light, Roger Smith, Tom Thorsen, Herb Golden, Jane Iselin, Lee Foster, Tom Morgan, and Mary Foster Morgan.

I am privileged to share with our Stony Hill neighbors, the DeCuevas family, a deep love for open fields, woodland, and most importantly, garlic. We have shared tractors, disc harrows, and seeders—and a similar affection for the land—with another neighbor, Randy Lerner. The stables owned and maintained by Wicketty Hotchkiss have added nourishment to our fields for fifteen years. And it has been a pleasure to work in the fields of north Amagansett for these many years with our fine neighbor Bob Strubel of Stony Hill Nursery. Jacques LeRolland, who serves faithfully as a master electrician and plumber, is also an accomplished, inventive, sly humorist; thank you to Sarah Donnelly as well. The "Green Thumb" family of Halseys has been kind to me since the first spring.

The Quail Hill Farm committee continues to improve the community as the farmers improve the soil structure. Four people have worked tirelessly, year after year: Jane Weissman, Gordian Raake, Nick Stephens, and Terry Stein. The beech trees of north Amagansett wept for the loss of Terry, sprouting seeds celebrate her. I thank Linda Lacchia for her spirit and energy, Hope Millholland, Arthur Kaliski, Sam Greico, Marilyn Lifshitz, Allen Sosne, Steve Frankel, and Hilary Leff for their humor, their ideas, and their enthusiasm. Edith and Alan Seligson have given a lot—I am most grateful for the gift of friendship and family.

A number of restaurant owners and chefs continue to be part of the Quail Hill Farm extended family. Leslie McEachern of Angelica Kitchen (corner of 12th Street and Second Avenue, New York City) was a most wonderful friend and resource in the early days of the farm. Colin Ambrose of Estia has been a brother in the field year after year; I admire his sincere love of food and farming, and also his generosity. It has been a delight to share the garden with everyone at Nick and Toni's, and I thank the chefs who have been kind to me one after another: Paul Del Favero, Joe Realmuto, and Seth Caswell. I also appreciate the support of Toni Ross, Mark Smith, Bonnie Munchin, Kirsten Benfield, and my composting comrade, Raul Banados. I would like to thank the entire crew of the Ross School kitchen, both past and present, especially Deena Chafetz, Beth Collins, and the most dedicated, informed, and delightful "lunch lady" I have yet to meet, Ann Cooper. Kristi Hood, now owner of the Springs General Store, has been kind to Quail Hill Farm, year after year.

It has been my privilege to share many afternoons with some very bright and sincere farmers and farm advocates, fellow members of the governing board of NOFA-NY: Alton Earnhart, Maureen Knapp, Mary Racinowski, Mary Jo Long, Vince Cirasole, Dick de Graff, Mark Dunau, Rex Farr, Wes Gillingham, David Hambleton, Liz Henderson, Trina Pilonero, Greg Schwartz, Stu McCarty, John Gorzinsky, Gary Skoog. Sarah Johnston steers the raft, and our collective work is enhanced by the dedication of Mayra Richter, Brian Caldwell, and Michael Gloss.

Although I am highly critical of the National Organic Program, I have nothing but praise for those who conduct the business of certification for NOFA-NY Certified Organic LLC: Carol King, Lisa Engelbert, and Amie Cristo.

I would like to express gratitude for the extraordinary work that they are doing to my Just Food friends: Kathy Lawrence, Joan Gussow, Ruth Katz, and Kristy Apostolides.

Virginia Farley and Peter Forbes, two land trust friends, each of whom happens to live in the Mad River valley of Vermont, have served as guides, and we have listened together to wind through the hardwoods, to water over stone, to wood cracking in the fire. I would like to thank Nancy Shea of the Murie Center, and Peter Forbes and Helen Whybrow of the Center for Whole Communities for providing place and space for thought and writing.

I have learned from several teachers who continue to spark my imagination and my writing: Milton Kessler, Basil Bunting, Chuck Matthei, Miriam McGillis, Peter Matthiessen, and my in-laws, Connie Fox and Bill King. I am always nourished by their example, their encouragement, and their artistic integrity.

Megan was nourished, as was I, by the exemplary lives of Dorothy and Pog Yglesias, who founded the Wild Bird Sanctuary in Mousehole. In reference to the link that can be made between humans and other creatures Dorothy wrote this: "It may be at that instant we go back to the awakening of all consciousness, making an intangible bridge of communication with every living thing."

I would like to acknowledge those with whom I shared timeless walks and conversation in Cornwall: Pete Perry, Sue Marshall, Liz and Tim Le Grice, Breon O'Casey, Andrew and Jackie Lanyon, Peter and Joan Hayes, Claire Lucas, Roger Davison, and Krysia Osostowicz.

This book would not exist without the insight and efforts of my agent and first editor, Paul Bresnick. Mary Bahr, formerly of Random House, was extremely generous with her seasoned advice and with her faith in my writing. And it has been a pleasure to work with my present editor at Viking, Paul Slovak. It was my good friend Don Lenzer who first suggested a book—thank you.

I have been lucky to share the farm work with a succession of savvy field managers often willing to arrive before the light, and to stay beyond the setting of the sun: Tim Laird, Paul Hamilton, Sarah Shapiro, Graham Hawks, and Matt Celona. And I want to thank Josh May, Rachel Daley, Abby Graseck, Evan Dick, and Nat Graeser for putting up with the farmer—with a deadline—glued to the computer screen at the end of each day.

Jessica Reynolds, whose drawings appear in these pages, first apprenticed at Quail Hill Farm in the year 2000; she reappears in Amagansett, with paper, pencils, chalk, and craypas, at least once a year. Her drawings—at one time a weekly revelation on the chalkboard at the Quail Hill farmstand—continue to have the impact of Charlotte's patterns within the web: Radiant.

Out of all this we have made a community farm. Finally, I would like to thank my family for their understanding and support. When eleven-year-old Liam, standing in the doorway to my study, soccer ball in hand, exclaimed, "I thought you already sent that book away!" I knew it was time to do just that. While I maintained the common ground for the community farm, Megan created harmony at home and for her sangha. Thank you, so much depends on you.

SOURCES

The following sources are listed in the order that they influence the story-teller and the story, beginning with the Introduction.

Shakespeare, William, *The Complete Pelican Shakespeare*, eds. Stephen Orgel and A. R. Braunmuiler (Penguin Books, 2002).

Yglesias, Dorothy, *The Cry of a Bird* (William Kimber, 1962).

Niedecker, Lorine, *T & G: The Collected Poems (1936–1966)* (The Jargon Society, 1968).

———, *The Granite Pail* (North Point Press, 1985).

Leopold, Aldo, *A Sand County Almanac* (Oxford University Press, 1966).

———, *The River of the Mother of God* (University of Wisconsin Press, 1991).

———, *For the Health of the Land* (Island Press, 1999).

Steindl-Rast, David, and Robert Aitken, *The Ground We Share* (Shambala, 1996).

Bunting, Basil, *Complete Poems* (New Directions, 2000).

Engeland, Ron, *Growing Great Garlic* (Filaree Productions, 1991).

Crawford, Stanley, *The Garlic Testament* (University of New Mexico Press, 1998).

The Garlic Press: www.garlicseedfoundation.info.

Sauer, Carl O., *Selected Essays, 1963–1975* (Turtle Island, 1981).

Fowles, John, "The Green Man," in *On Nature*, ed. Daniel Halpern (North Point Press, 1987).

Sophocles, *Antigone*, in *The Complete Greek Tragedies*, ed. David Greene and Richmond Lattimore (University of Chicago Press, 1992).

Bishop, Elizabeth, *Geography III* (Farrar, Straus and Giroux, 1978).

———, *The Complete Poems* (Farrar, Straus and Giroux, 1969).

Hay, John, *The Undiscovered Country* (W. W. Norton, 1982), p. 12: "In other words, during our lifetimes, we share in the unending changing facets of the sentient earth. . . ."

Hopkins, Gerard Manley, *A Hopkins Reader* (Doubleday, 1966).

Oppen, George, *Of Being Numerous* (New Directions, 1968).

Keats, John, *Complete Poetical Works and Letters* (Houghton Mifflin, 1899).

Dickinson, Emily, "Final Harvest," in *Emily Dickinson's Poems* (Little, Brown, 1961).

Joyce, James, *Finnegans Wake* (Viking Press, 1939).

Grahame, Kenneth, *The Wind in the Willows* (Henry Holt, 1980).

Whitman, Walt, *Poetry and Prose* (Library of America, 1982).

Heaney, Seamus, *Seeing Things* (Farrar, Straus and Giroux, 1991).

———, *Field Work* (Farrar, Straus and Giroux, 1979).

Howard, Sir Albert, *An Agricultural Testament* (Oxford University Press, 1940).

———, *The Soil and Health* (Schocken Books, 1947).

Balfour, Lady Eve, *The Living Soil and the Haughley Experiment* (Faber and Faber, 1975).

King, Franklin H., *Farmers of Forty Centuries* (1911; Rodale Press, 1973).

Cooper, Ann, *Bitter Harvest* (Routledge, 2000).

Williams, Carol, *Bringing a Garden to Life* (Bantam, 1998).

Storl, W. D., *Culture and Horticulture* (Bio-Dynamic Literature, 1979).

Wordsworth, William, *Selected Poems* (Penguin Books, 1994).

Kessler, Milton, *Free Concert* (Etruscan Press, 2002).

———, *The Grand Concourse* (MSS Press, 1990).

Whynott, Douglas, *Following the Bloom* (Beacon Press, 1991).

Hubbell, Sue, *A Book of Bees* (Houghton Mifflin, 1988).

Steiner, Rudolf, *Bees* (Anthroposophic Press, 1998).

Hauk, Gunther, *Towards Saving the Honeybee* (B-D Association, 2002).

Yeats, W. B., *Collected Poems* (Macmillan, 1970).

Frost, Robert. *Collected Poems, Prose, and Plays* (Library of America, 1995).

Snyder, Gary, *The Practice of the Wild* (North Point Press, 1990).

———, *A Place in Space* (Counterpoint, 1995).

Montale, Eugenio, *Poesie,* transl. George Kay (Edinburgh University Press, 1964).

———, *Mottetti,* transl. Dana Gioia (Graywolf Press, 1990).

Gioia, Dana, and William Jay Smith, eds., *Poems from Italy* (New Rivers Press, 1985).

Schwenke, Karl, *Successful Small-Scale Farming: An Organic Approach* (Storey Communications, 1995).

Williams, Terry Tempest, "The Open Space of Democracy," in *Orion* (March–April through July–August 2004).

Van En, Robyn, *Basic Formula to Create Community Supported Agriculture* (Indian Line Farm, 1988).

Henderson, Elizabeth, with Robyn Van En, *Sharing the Harvest* (Chelsea Green, 1999).

Smith, Miranda, ed., *The Real Dirt* (Sustainable Agriculture Publications, 1994).

Bowman, Greg, ed., *Steel in the Field* (Sustainable Agriculture Network, 1997).

Grubinger, Vernon P., *Sustainable Vegetable Production from Start-up to Market* (NRAES, 1999).

Southern Exposure Seed Exchange, gardens@southernexposure.com.

White, E. B., *One Man's Meat* (Tilbury House, 1997).

Makhanlall, David P., *The Best of Brer Anansi* (Blackie and Son, 1973).

Smith, William Jay, *The Traveler's Tree* (Persea Books, 1980).

Pyle, Robert Michael, *Chasing Monarchs: Migrating with the Butterflies of Passage* (Mariner Books, 2001).

Nabhan, Gary Paul, *The Forgotten Pollinators* (Island Press, 1996).

Silverstein, Alvin and Virginia, *Life in a Bucket of Soil* (Dover, 2000).

Kimbrell, Andrew, ed., *The Fatal Harvest Reader* (Island Press, 2002).

Fukuoka, Masanobu, *The One-Straw Revolution* (Rodale Press, 1978).

Bailey, Liberty Hyde, *The Holy Earth* (Macmillan, 1905).

Gliessman, Stephen, *Agroecology: Ecological Processes in Sustainable Agriculture* (Ann Arbor Press, 1998).

Logan, William Bryant, "Hans Jenny at the Pygmy Forest," in *Orion* (Spring 1992).

Farb, Peter, *Living Earth* (Harper and Row, 1959).

Magdoff, Fred, *Building Soils for Better Crops* (University of Nebraska Press, 1992).

Smillie, Joe, and Grace Gershuny, *The Soul of Soil* (Chelsea Green, 1999).

Thompkins, Peter, and Christopher Bird, *Secrets of the Soil* (Harper and Row, 1989).

Selden, George, *The Cricket in Times Square* (Dell 1960).

Murie, Olaus and Mardy, *Wapiti Wilderness* (University of Colorado Press, 1985).

Pound, Ezra, *The Cantos* (New Directions, 1972).

Matthiessen, Peter, *The Wind Birds* (Chapters Publishing, 1994).

———, *Wildlife in America* (Viking, 1959).

Berry, Wendell, *What Are People For?* (North Point Press, 1990).

———, *Collected Poems* (North Point Press, 1985).

———, *The Unsettling of America* (Avon, 1977).

Blake, William, *The Complete Poetry and Prose of William Blake*, ed. David Erdman (Doubleday, 1968).

Rilke, Rainer Maria, *Ahead of All Parting: The Selected Poetry and Prose* (Modern Library 1995).

Pollan, Michael, *The Botany of Desire* (Random House, 2001).

Gass, William H., *Reading Rilke* (Knopf, 1999).

Cobbett, William (series ed. Michael Pollan), *The American Gardener* (Modern Library, 2003).

Gussow, Joan Dye, *This Organic Life* (Chelsea Green, 2001).

E. F. Schumacher, *Small Is Beautiful* (Anchor Press, 1973).

Jackson, Wes, *Becoming Native to This Place* (University of Kentucky Press, 1994).

———, *Call for a Revolution in Agriculture* (E. F. Schumacher Society, 1981).

Abram, David, *The Spell of the Sensuous* (Vintage Books, 1996).

The Earth Charter: www.earthcharter.org.

Bubel, Mike and Nancy, *Root Cellaring* (Garden Way, 1992).

Small Farmer's Journal, Lynn R. Miller, editor.

Tucker, David M., *Kitchen Gardening in America: A History* (Iowa State University Press, 1993).

Waters, Charles, and C. J. Fenzau, *Eco-Farm* (Acres USA, 1996).

Newman, Nell, with Joseph D'Agnese, *The Newman's Own Organics Guide to a Good Life* (Villard, 2003).

Williams, W. C., *The Collected Poems of William Carlos Williams: 1909–1939, Vol. 1* (New Directions, 1991).

Ashworth, Susan, *Seed to Seed* (Seed Savers Exchange, 1991).

Seed Savers Exchange Yearbook (Seed Savers Exchange, Decorah, Iowa; updated each year).

Morrow, Susan Brind, *The Names of Things* (Riverhead Books, 1997).

Ross, Nancy Wilson, *Three Ways of Asian Wisdom* (Simon and Schuster, 1969).

Peattie, Donald Culross, *Flowering Earth* (Indiana University Press, 1991).

Wilson, Edward O., *The Diversity of Life* (Harvard University Press, 1992).

Shiva, Vandana, *Stolen Harvest* (South End Press, 2000).

Holdrege, Craig, *Genetics and the Manipulation of Life* (Lindisfarne Press, 1996).

Stella Natura. B-D Farming and Gardening Association. www.camphill kimberton.org.

Geisler, Charles, and Gail Daneker, eds., *Property and Values* (Island Press, 2000).

Elder, John, *Reading the Mountains of Home* (Harvard University Press, 1998).

———, *The Frog Run* (Milkweed Editions, 2001).

Savory, Allen, *Holistic Resource Management* (Island Press, 1991).

Forbes, Peter, *The Great Remembering* (The Trust for Public Land, 2001).

———, *Our Land, Ourselves* (The Trust for Public Land, 1999).

Lappé, Frances Moore, and Anna Lappé, *Hope's Edge* (Jeremy P. Tarcher / Putnam, 2002).

The author would like to draw the reader's attention to the Land Ethic Toolbox, www.wilderness.org, a valuable piece of work contributed by Robert Perschel. For those interested in a further search, the following books—also listed above—offer informative, well-researched resource pages: *Sharing the Harvest; Sustainable Vegetable Production from Start-up to Market; The Newman's Own Guide; The Fatal Harvest Reader;* and *Hope's Edge.*